A
XVth Century Guide-Book
TO THE
Principal Churches of Rome

AMS PRESS
NEW YORK

et in illa sunt multe indulgencie. In Capella
que est hic eciam in curia ubi sunt colune de
alabastro sunt infinite indulgencie et in illa
est studium beati Gregorii et erat tota ornata
musayco :· Reliquie in Capella Salvatoris

Capella salvatoris seu sancti laurencii
ab antiquo vocata in sacro palacio lateranensi
ibi est ymago salvatoris quam sanctus lucas
colores non imposuit ut patet et scriptura presente &c.
Preciosissima pignora ibi requiescunt tam in
dominum salvatorem cuius laudabile ibi notat ymago
quam et beatorum apostolorum inter quos confessor et virginum que
fere omnes in archa quadam cupressina requiescunt
quam leo tercius misit fieri & ut supra ...
existentem infra ipsum altare beati laurencii cum
aliis diuinis pignoribus collocauit sunt autem
in ea tres casse in vna quarum que in modum
crucis est facta extat crux de auro preciosissimo
decorata iacinctis smaragdis et prasinis et in
medio crucis huius est passio uidelicet dominum nostrum
Ihesum Christum Reliquie circuciscionis passionis Ihesu Christi et ipso
sacro loco erat & omnis pontifex de ipso decorauit

Folio 17b.
Reliquie in Capella Salvatoris in Palacio Lateranensi.

A
XVth Century Guide-Book
TO THE
Principal Churches of Rome

Compiled C. 1470 by

WILLIAM BREWYN

TRANSLATED FROM THE LATIN
with introduction and notes

by

C. EVELEIGH WOODRUFF, M.A.

HON. LIBRARIAN TO THE DEAN AND CHAPTER OF CANTERBURY

Non tantum isse juvat Romam bene vivere quantum
Vel Romae, vel ubi vita agitur hominis
Non via credo pedum, sed morum ducit ad astra
Quisquid ubique gerit, spectat ab arce Deus.

(Theodulf of Orleans).

THE MARSHALL PRESS, LIMITED,
7, MILFORD LANE, STRAND, LONDON, W.C.2
1933

Library of Congress Cataloging in Publication Data

Berwyn, William, fl. 1470.
  A XVth century guide-book to the principal churches
of Rome.

  Reprint of the 1933 3d. published by the Marshall
Press, London.
  "XVth cent. English poems": p.
  Includes index.
  1. Rome (City)—Churches.   I. Woodruff, Charles
Eveleigh, 1855 or 6-   II. Title.
BX1548.R6B73   1980   282'.45632   78-63451
ISBN 0-404-16374-2

Reprinted from the edition of 1933, London. Trim size has
been altered (original: 14 × 21.5 cm). Text area is un-
changed.

MANUFACTURED
IN THE UNITED STATES OF AMERICA

INTRODUCTION

THE medieval Guide book to the principal churches of the City of Rome—of which an English translation is here given for the first time—was purchased from a London bookseller by the Dean and Chapter of Canterbury in 1922, and is now preserved in their library (Press mark Z.8.33). It is a duodecimo volume of 101 vellum leaves measuring 140 x 97 mm., in an eighteenth century binding of rough calf. The contents throughout appear to be written by one hand in a script characteristic of the second half of the fifteenth century. The initial letters are illuminated in blue with marginal scroll-work executed with the pen in red.

On the first leaf, in a hand of about the same period as the binding, is the following inscription :

" *This Manuscript was writ by William Brewyn Chantry Priest at St. Thomas' Shrine in Christchurch in Canterbury Anᵒ 1477 (No. 32).*"

There is, however, nothing in the book which corroborates the above statement. The author describes himself merely as William Brewyn, chaplain, that is, he was an unbeneficed secular priest, and as a secular he could not have been connected with the altar of the shrine of St. Thomas, which was always served by the Christchurch monks.

All that appears to be known about William Brewyn is to be found in Casimir Oudin's *Commentarium de Scriptoribus Ecclesiasticis* (Leipsic 1722).

Oudin states that Brewyn, or Brevin, was an Englishman who, during the pontificates of Paul II and Sixtus IV lived for many years in Rome, where he became well known as a diligent investigator of the antiquities of the City, and was the author of a little book of some merit (*opusculum non contemnendum*) on the Seven Principal Churches of Rome, a copy of

B

which, Oudin adds, in his day was preserved in the Vatican Library. A careful search, however, of the catalogues in the MSS. room of the Vatican library— (which was kindly undertaken for me by Dr. Annie Cameron, of the British School at Rome) failed to discover any reference to Brewyn's book, nor is it mentioned in Forcella's catalogue of MSS. in the Vatican relating to the history of Rome, which was published in 1879.

As to the provenance of the Canterbury copy, though nothing was revealed at the time of its purchase, there can be no doubt whatever that it came from the library of Sir Henry Ingilby, of Ripley Castle, Yorks. The Ripley manuscripts are described in the Sixth Report of the Historical MSS. Commissioners— (issued in 1877)—and amongst them is William Brewyn's guide to the Seven Principal Churches of Rome, with an inscription on its first page identical with that quoted above.

Since the writer of the above Report states that many of the Ripley MSS. are supposed to have come from Fountain's Abbey, and Bridlington Priory, Brewyn's book may have been among them ; possibly it had been deposited in one of the above named religious houses by a pious Yorkshireman on his return from a pilgrimage to the eternal city.

Certainly it would have been a useful guide for a pilgrim to have in his wallet, for besides detailed information about the holy places of Rome it gives practical advice as to the journey thither.

With regard to date ; it is reasonable to suppose that the topographical part of the book was compiled during the author's stay in Rome. He was certainly there in 1469 when Pope Paul II pronounced excommunication against all persons who should molest pilgrims coming to the holy city, for he tells us he made a copy of the bull when it was fixed to the door of the church of St. Peter ; but in the following year, he tells us he was in Canterbury during the celebration of the jubilee of St. Thomas.

But although Brewyn wrote in the second half of the fifteenth century, by which time the New Learning had made considerable progress—at any rate in Italy—and already by scholars had been applied to the criticism of such legends as the Donation of Constantine, his work shows no indication of such influence. He repeats the most extravagant of these legends with the same unquestioning faith as his predecessors had done, of whom the most famous was a certain Master Gregory whose *Mirabilia Urbis Romae* was for more than four centuries the standard book on the topography of Rome[1].

The *Mirabilia* which, according to Gregorovius, can be traced back to the second half of the tenth century[1] was printed by Montfaucon, in 1702 in his *Diarium Italicum,* and several critical editions have been published more recently, notably that of Urlichs in his *Codex Urbis Romae Topographicus.* An English version of the *Mirabilia* was published in 1889 by Francis Morgan Nichols who has incorporated therewith a translation of another little treatise entitled *Mirabiliana,* or Marvels of the Churches of Rome, which, according to Nichols, was compiled in 1375. Both works were known and used by Brewyn, but whereas the earlier writers merely enumerate the holy places, he assigns to each its exact spiritual value expressed in terms of Indulgences. To each church, shrine or station a definite Indulgence is attached, it may be of forty days or forty thousand years, but

---

[1] Portions of still earlier Guides or Itineraries are extant viz. The Itinerary of Wurtzbourg *De locis sanctorum martyrum quae sunt foris civitatis Romae,* and the Itinerary of Salzbourg, *Notitia ecclesiarum urbis Romae,* both of which date back to the seventh century. See Dict. *D'Archeologie Chretienne.* Art. *Itineraires.*

William of Malmesbury in *Gesta Regum Anglorum* gives a topographical account of Rome in the twelfth century. Ed. T. Duffus Hardy, vol. ii, pp. 539-544.

Brewyn, who presumably drew his information from the *Libri Indulgentiarum*[1] always states with meticulous care the exact extent of the privilege.

The granting of Indulgences is a controversial subject into which it is unnecessary to enter here ; it will be sufficient to state that the practice was founded on the belief that the merits of the Lord Christ and His saints constituted an infinite treasure on which Christ's vicar by the power of the keys might draw ; and by theologians an Indulgence is defined as a remission of the temporal punishment due to sins remitted as to their guilt in the sacrament of penance, though what proportion of temporal punishment, or what duration in purgatory would correspond to a penance of one hundred days or years has never been defined.

There can be little doubt, however, that to the ordinary medieval mind the phrase *remissio omnium peccatorum* which accompanied the plenary Indulgence meant a good deal more than the mere remission of temporal punishment. That there was discrepancy between the authorized teaching of the Church and popular belief on the subject of Indulgences was at length recognised, with the result that the system was revised and regulated by the Council of Trent in 1553. The granting of special Indulgences at the time of the papal jubilees does not appear to have been in use before the time of Boniface VIII, (1294-1303) who, in his constitution *De Paenitentiis et Remissionibus in communibus*, declared an Indulgence on the recurrence of the hundredth year to all who, being truly penitent and confessed, should visit devoutly the basilican churches of Rome[2].

[1] Forty editions of the *Libri Indulgentiae* were printed between 1489 and 1524, see Oscar Pollak's *Le Guide Di Roma*, edited by Ludwig Schudt, Vienna, 1930. It is noteworthy that Le Guide Di Roma does not mention Brewyn's work.

[2] See Van Espen, *Jus Ecclesiasticum Universum*, vol. ii, Cap. vi, p. 235. The interval between the jubilees was reduced to fifty years by Clement VI in 1350 ; to thirty-three years by Urban VI in 1388 ; and to twenty-five years by Paul II in 1470.

Brewyn however, attributes to St. Gregory the granting of Indulgences connected with ' Stations ' though there is no evidence whatever of their existence until many centuries later[1], and the plenary Indulgences of the Lateran Church he even refers back to St. Silvester, though to attribute to them such antiquity is purely fantastical[2].

Further proof of credulity is to be found in Brewyn's repetition of the ridiculous story that the Pope, on the day of his enthronement, had to submit to an absurd and shameful investigation for the purpose of proving he was a man.

The story—which of course had its origin in the myth that a woman, in the person of Pope Joan, had once occupied the chair of St. Peter (she was supposed to have succeeded Leo IV in 855),—had been current in Rome since the thirteenth century, and is to be found in the Mirabiliana.

Von Döllinger in his *Fables respecting the Popes in the Middle Ages* gives the following explanation of the ceremony : " It was the custom," he writes, " from the time of Paschal II, in the year 1099, at the solemn procession to the Lateran, for the new pope to sit down on two pierced seats made of stone . . . These seats dated from the times of ancient Rome, and had formerly stood, it appears, in one of the public baths . . . Here it was usual for the Pope to sit first on the right hand seat, while a girdle from which hung seven seals and seven keys, was put round him, at the same time a staff was placed in his hand, which he, then sitting on the left hand seat, placed along with the keys in the hands of the prior of St. Laurence[3]. Leo X is said to have been the last pope to sit on these seats.

---

[1] *Ibid*, vol. ii, p. 228.

[2] *Indulgentiae plenariae quae a Silvestro concesisse dicuntur visitantibus ecclesiam Lateranensem nullum apud eruditos fidem merentur*, *ibid*, vol. ii, p. 230.

[3] *Op. cit ;* trans. by Plummer, p. 48. Nichols gives a somewhat different explanation of the ceremony. "The Pope," he says, "while seated in the first seat, received the keys of the Lateran palace, and from the second threw money to the people." *Mirabilia ut supra*, p. 130.

At the end of his description of the holy places
Brewyn has inserted a copy of the Bull of Pope Paul II
excommunicating all persons who should attack, or
in any way molest, pilgrims on their journey to Rome,
or during their stay in the city. He was present, he
tells us, when the Bull was read at the door of the
Church of St. Peter on Maundy Thursday in the year
1469, and he made a copy of the instrument which
after the ceremony was attached to the door of the
church. The knowledge that some steps had been
taken to ensure their safety would give confidence to
those who might be contemplating making a pilgrimage to the eternal city, so Brewyn inserts the Bull
as a sort of insurance policy.

He then proceeds to give some practical advice
concerning the journey.

Writing as an Englishman for Englishmen he
begins his itinerary at Calais ; but since war between
England and France was threatening, if it had not
already broken out, the pilgrim is recommended to
travel by way of the Netherlands, Germany, and the
Tyrol into Lombardy and thence to Rome. For those
who might desire to avoid passing through Cologne,
where the Bishop was in the habit of levying a poll
tax on all travellers, an alternative route is suggested
whereby the imposition might be escaped by taking
the road through Trier and Speyer to Trent.

The distances between the various stages are noted,
but Brewyn's miles (*milliaria*) correspond more nearly
to leagues than to English miles.

Notes on the towns through which the pilgrim
would pass are added, with occasional warnings of
dangers which might be encountered on the road ;
information as to the various kinds of money required ;
and the accommodation afforded by the inns. Of the
innkeepers of Bonn Brewyn seems to have had un-
pleasant recollections, for he exclaims in his native

tongue, " Here be fals shrewys[1] summe " adding—
more charitably—in Latin, " *Nisi meliorantur.*"

The Itinerary is followed by a Table of Exchange of
divers kinds of money—a complicated document—
about which it may be sufficient here to state that
Brewyn received in Rome two ducats in exchange for
nine shillings of English money, and that he recom-
mends pilgrims to be well supplied with papal groats,
bemys, blaffords, crucers, and Cologne pence, since
these will be found the most useful coins for the
journey. The next fifty-three leaves contain an account
of the Roads, Bridges and Triumphal Arches of Rome,
followed by Legends of the Saints, but since the former
is copied, sometimes almost verbally, from the
Polichronicon of Ranulf Higden and the *Mirabilia*, and
the latter from the *Legenda Aurea* of Jacobus de
Voragine[2] I have omitted this portion of the work.
The Legends of the Saints now end with the story of
St. Giles ; but from the table of contents at the
beginning of the book we learn that here should
follow an account of a pilgrimage to the Holy Land.
Unfortunately the leaf containing it has been cut out,
a loss which is all the more regrettable from the fact
that, according to the Table, part of the account was
written in English.

On folios 95 and 96 Brewyn has inserted a list of
the Relics in the Cathedral Church of Christ in
Canterbury which—by the way—he calls the " Church
of St. Thomas, the Archprelate." He compiled the
inventory, he tells us, when he was in Canterbury in
1470, during the celebration of the sixth jubilee of St.
Thomas.

Compared with the great Inventory of Canterbury
Relics,—compiled in 1315, during the priorate of
Henry of Eastry, and printed in Legg and Hope's

---

[1] Shrew originally signified a vexatious person of either sex. O.E.D.

[2] Brewyn acknowledges his indebtedness, e.g. " *Haec in Policronica Cestrie
libro primo.*" " *Item Gregorii in originali de mirabilibus Romae,*" etc.

Inventories of Christ Church, Canterbury[1], Brewyn's list appears a somewhat meagre document, many things mentioned in the earlier inventory being omitted from the later one, though there are a few additions. For instance, whereas in Eastry's list the *Corpora Sanctorum* include those of twelve saints only, Brewyn doubles their number by including the *Corpora* of a number of Anglo-Saxon archbishops, and the body of St. Syburgis, sometime Abbess of Minster in Thanet. That he was unfamiliar with the history of the church of Canterbury is clear from his vague reference to Archbishop Odo, whose anniversary was kept at Canterbury as a semi-double, as " a saint who is *called* Odo ! "

Further additions to the earlier list are : A part of the seamless coat of the Saviour, St. Mary Magdalene's alabaster box, something called the *pome* of St. Thomas, and an arm of St. Osmund, Bishop of Salisbury. The last was a recent acquisition, having been brought to Canterbury by brothers John Newton and John Newbery who had been appointed by the prior and convent of Christ Church to represent them at the translation of St. Osmund (July 23rd, 1457)[2]. On the last leaves of the volume (98-101) are certain religious poems in English, written, apparently, by the same hand as the previous part of the book. Though of no great literary merit these poems are interesting as specimens of English versification at a period about midway between the age of Chaucer and that of the Elizabethan poets.

* * *

In making the translation from the Latin the aim has been to give a literal interpretation of the text. A few notes have been added ; but in view of the number of works already in existence dealing with the ecclesiastical antiquities of Rome, no attempt has been made to comment exhaustively upon the subject in this little volume.

[1] From Cottonian MS. Galba E. IV B.M.
[2] See *Stone's Chronicle*, Ed. Searle, p. 71.

[Translation].

A TABLE OF THIS BOOK.

In this little book a description is given of the seven principal churches of the city of Rome, as is set forth below,—and of certain relics and indulgences which are contained therein.*

Other churches are described also which are not among these principal ones, namely : the church called St. Mary the New ; the church of St. Mary on the other side of the bridge (*transpontina*), the church of St. Mary Round, the church of St. Peter's Chains, the church of St. John before the Latin gate, the church of St. Silvester, the church of St. James, the church of St. Praxedes, the church of St. Potenciana (*sic*), and the church of St. Bartholomew, the apostle.

Also, something is said about the Stations at Rome both within and without (the walls), and the days on which they are made. Also, concerning the church of St. Peter in Carcere ; the chapel called " Scala cœli " ; the cemetery of Calixtus ; a further account of the indulgences and relics belonging to the church of St. John Lateran, according to what I found written there, to wit, those pertaining to the high altar, and to the tabernacle nearest to it, and to the greater tabernacle, and to the inner chapel,—as is set forth below. Also, concerning the relics and indulgences of the church at the font of Constantine.

Also concerning the relics in the chapel called the Saviour's, or Laurence's chapel, and the wonderful vision there. Also, a further account of the church of St. Peter, the Apostle.

*Fo. 2a.

Also, concerning the church of Pudenciana, and the relics and other things there.

Also, concerning the church of St. Paul, the Apostle, where the monks of the order of St. Benedict have their abode, and the relics and indulgences, according to what I found written there.

Also, there is much about the church of St. Mary of the People.

Also, concerning the church called the Altar of Heaven (*Ara Coeli*) where I found many inscriptions on tablets (*tabulis*) relating to relics, indulgences, etc.*

Also, concerning the chapel called *Scala coeli*, at the three fountains ; and the church of the Holy Cross with its relics and indulgences.

Also, concerning the Jerusalem chapel, which is behind the altar of the same church.

Also, concerning the church of SS. Sebastian and Fabian, and its relics and indulgences ; the church of St. Clement and its relics and indulgences, the church of St. Bartholomew and its relics and indulgences, the church of St. Cecilia and its relics and indulgences.

Also, concerning certain excommunications which Pope Paul pronounced through two cardinals,—as is set forth below.

Also, concerning the route (*via*) from Calais to Rome, as traversed by me.

Also, about the exchange and divers kinds of money.

Also, concerning the streets of the city of Rome, and divers places and gates.

Also, concerning the site of the City of Rome ; its hills, bridges, and the palaces which formerly were part of the same city.

Also, concerning the triumphal arches ; the wonders of Rome (mirabilibus), and the saints who rest in divers roads and places, according to what is contained in the martyrology, to wit, in the Appian and

*Fo. 2b.

Salarian ways, etc., as is set forth below, together with an account of some other things which are generally described at Rome.

Also, concerning the histories and legends of the saints of Rome, to wit, about the birth of Christ; St. Anastasia, a very noble Roman lady, and her three chaste girls ; St. Sylvester and how he shut the dragon's mouth ; St. Fabian and St. Sebastian.

Also, concerning the great concourse of people who came to the dedication of the church of St. Sebastian ; the plague in Italy in the time of King Gubert[1] (*sic*, for Gumbert) the temptation of Paulinus and his acts ; Paula, a noble matron.

Also, concerning the blessed apostle Peter and what happened to him when he preached at Antioch.

Also, concerning the river called the mouth of the Tiber.

Also, concerning the meeting of Abbot John with the blessed Pope Gregory.

Also, concerning St. Gregory celebrating in the church of St. Mary the Greater.

Also, concerning a certain wealthy Roman who left his wife, and what he did for St. Gregory, the Pope. Also, about Tiberius Cæsar, Veronica, Pontius Pilate, the judge of Christ, St. Ambrose's journey to Rome and the holy places, the excommunication that Pope Marcellinus promulgated against those who should bury him.[2]

St. Pancras and how perjurers were treated by him, Pope Urban, and the persecution of the church in his time.

Also, concerning St. Petronilla, the daughter of the blessed Peter the Apostle ; St. Leo, the Pope, cele-

---

[1]The pestilence in Italy is recorded by Paul the deacon in *De Gestis Langobardorum*—Muratori *Rerum Italicorum Scriptores* Vol. 1, p. 426.

[2]During the Diocletian persecution Marcellinus offered incense to the Roman gods, and therefore judged himself unworthy of Christian burial.

brating mass in the church of St. Mary the greater, on the day of the Resurrection, etc.*

St. Peter and his miracles, according to the Golden Legend.

St. Paul the apostle, and the finding of his head.

Also, concerning Eudosia, daughter of the emperor Theodosius, to whom a Jew gave the chain of St. Peter the apostle ; and the conjunction (*conjunctio*) of the holy bodies of saints Stephen and Laurence[1].

Also, concerning St. Dominic, and the grace of the Virgin Mary, etc. ; the blessed Laurence and certain of his miracles, to wit, the one about a holy nun, and a priest who was repairing a church ; also about Stephen, the judge, and the heretical emperor, etc.

Also, concerning SS. Hypolitus and Subulcus, as they were driving a wagon on St. Mary Magdalene's day ; St. Felix, the pope, and how he built churches (*sic*) in honour of SS. Cosmas and Damian ; the fire at Rome in the time of Pope Calixtus ; and the Temple, dedicated in honour of All Saints.

Also, concerning the story of the keeper of the church of St. Peter ; the most illustrious virgin St. Cecilia ; St. Clement the Pope, and how his body came to Rome ; St. Giles, and the grace which the king received from him and through him was granted to others[2].

*Fo. 3b.

[1]In A.D. 445 the Greeks agreed to exchange the body of St. Stephen, the protomartyr, for that of St. Laurence. When the body of St. Stephen was brought to Rome from Constantinople, a girl who was possessed by a devil proclaimed that the Saint wished to share the tomb of his brother Laurence, and when his bones were brought thither, Laurence obligingly made room for him by shifting his position and leaving a vacant place by his side into which the body of Stephen was deposited. When the Greeks attempted to remove the body of Laurence they were unable to do so, and a voice from heaven was heard saying, " O, happy Rome, which possesses in one tomb the bodies of Laurence of Spain, and Stephen of Jerusalem."

[2]The book ends with the legend of St. Giles, certain leaves having been cut out after folio 39b ; what follows in the Table is not now to be found in the book.

Also, concerning a pilgrimage to the Holy Land, and to the following places :—Nazareth, Jerusalem, the Church of the Holy Sepulchre, Mount Sion, Acheldama, the valley of Josephat, (*sic*) the Temple of the Lord, Bethlehem, Bethany, the river Jordan, Jericho, the desert mountain of Galgala, the city of Kaer, Alexandria, Caesarea in Palestine, Acra, Tybirias, Arabia, Tyre and Sydon, Baruta and other places in the Holy Land and elsewhere. Also some particulars of the Stations of Jerusalem and of the Holy Land are given in English for those who may desire to visit the Holy Land with the devout intention of acquiring indulgences,—according to what I found in a roll (*in rotula*)[1].

THE CHURCH OF ST. JOHN LATERAN.*

Saint Silvester, the Pope, asserts in his Chronicle that there were one thousand five hundred and five churches at Rome of which the greater number are now no longer in use (*desolatae*). Amongst these churches there are seven to which special privileges are attached, and these seven are called the royal churches, because they were built by kings and princes. The first church is the church of St. John Lateran[2]. Now in this church, every day there are xlviii years of indulgences, and as many quarantines (*quadragenae*)[3], and remission of the third part of all sins.

Also, Pope Silvester, and Pope Gregory, who consecrated the same church, granted here such great

---

[1]Dom Le Clercq mentions a MS of the XIV cent. in the form of a roll in the monastery of St. Gall in which the *Mirabilia Urbis Romae* is followed by a list of the Indulgences of the chief churches of Rome. *Dict. D'Archeologie Chretienne. Art. Itineraires.*

*Fo. 5a.

[2]This is copied from the Liber Indulgentiae, *see* Ludwig Schudk's, Le Guide de Roma p. 185.

[3]A fast of 40 successive days.

indulgences that no one can count them—they are known to God only ; and these (indulgences) Pope Boniface[1] confirmed, declaring that if men knew how great were the indulgences of the church of St. John Lateran, they would not cross over to the Sepulchre of the Lord in Jerusalem, nor to St. James in Compostella.

Also, the Pope declared that if anyone shall draw nigh to our throne (*sedem*) in the Lateran, for worship, prayer, or pilgrimage, he shall be cleansed from all his sins. Pope Boniface said also, that if anyone shall come to the aforesaid church on the dedication festival, and shall there devoutly pray, he shall obtain remission of all his sins. In the Sacristy of the same church is the altar of St. John, which he had in the desert ; the ark of the covenant ; the table at which our Lord supped with His disciples ; and the rod of Moses and Aaron, all of which Titus, and Vespasian, brought from Jerusalem, together with the four brazen columns which stand round the high altar, and, over (*super*) the high altar are the heads of the apostles Peter and Paul,*; and whensoever these are shown, then the indulgences are as great as they are in the churches of Peter and Paul, when the face of our Lord Jesus Christ is shown[2].

Also, in the chapel of St. John, into which women may not enter, there is remission of all sins.

Also, in the chapel which is called the Holy of Holies (*Sancta Sanctorum*), into which women do not enter, there is plenary remission of all sins. Here, also, is a picture (*imago*) of our Lord Jesus Christ as He was at the age of twelve years.

[1]Boniface VIII.

*Fo. 5b.

[2]The heads of SS. Peter and Paul were removed from the chapel of St. Laurence (*Sancta Sanctorum*) to the high altar of the Lateran church by Pope Urban V in 1367.

THE CHURCH OF ST. PETER[1].

The second church is the church of St. Peter in which every day there are xlviii years of indulgences, and as many quarantines, and the remission of a third part of all sins.

Also, in the same church there used to be one hundred and eleven altars which now, for the most part, are destroyed, and, at each one, twenty-eight years of indulgence.

Also, when it is the feast of any of the said altars, or the feast of St. Peter, the Nativity of our Lord, Easter, All Saints, and, on other double feasts, these indulgences are doubled to all persons who shall visit the church on the aforesaid festivals.

Also, there are seven altars of special rank (*maiori dignitate*), to wit, the altars of the Blessed Virgin Mary ; St. Veronica, of St. Andrew, of St. Leo, the Pope, St. Gregory, and SS. Simon and Jude.*

Also, on the day of the Lord's Supper, and on the feast of the Annunciation of the Blessed Virgin Mary, there are a thousand years of indulgences.

Also, from the said feast to the Kalends of August there are a thousand years of indulgences, and as many quarantines, and the remission of a third part of all sins.

Also, whensoever anyone shall go up the steps of St. Peter's for worship, prayer or pilgrimage, for every step eight years of indulgences are granted[2].

[1]According to the *Liber Pontificalis* the church of St. Peter was built by the Emperor Constantine at the request of Pope Sylvester—Pope Damasus added a baptistery, A.D. 366.

Marucchi states that in 1450 the church was in such a bad state that the pilgrims who came to the jubilee of that year were much shocked. The new church was commenced by Nicholas (1447-1455), but not much was done until the time Pope Julius II (1503-1513).

*Fo. 6a.

[2]A flight of 35 steps led up to the atrium from the piazza below.

Also, in the aforesaid church, repose viii bodies of the apostles ; also one half of the bodies of Peter and Paul lieth at Peter's, but the other half lieth at St. Paul's[1] ; the bodies of SS. Simon and Jude, and the body of St. John Crisostim (*sic*) ; also the bodies of the martyrs Processus and Martinian ; the body of St. Petronilla, the Virgin ; the head of St. Andrew[2] and his arm ; the head of St. Sebastian ; the head of St. Luke the evangelist.

Also, whensoever the face of our Lord Jesus Christ is shown there are three thousand years of indulgences, that is to say, those who live near Rome have six thousand years of indulgences, and those who come over the mountains and hills have nine thousand years of indulgences, and as many quarantines, and the remission of a third part of all sins.

THE CHURCH OF ST. PAUL*[3]

The third church is the church of St. Paul, and every day at the high altar xlviii years of indulgence are granted and as many quarantines and the remission of a third part of all sins.

Also, on the feast of the Conversion of St. Paul there are a hundred years of indulgences, and as many quarantines, and the remission of a third part of all sins ; on the feast of the Holy Innocents there are xliiii

[1]Until about the middle of the IXth century the Roman church was opposed to the division of the bodies of Saints and their distribution to various churches.

[2]The head of St. Andrew was brought to Rome in 1462 by the last of the Palaeologi to save it from the Turks and was placed in the church of St. Peter by Pope Pius II. *See* Creighton's History of the Papacy, Vol. II, pp. 436, 438.

*Fo. 6b.

[3]The church of St. Paul, outside the walls, was built by Pope Sylvester on the Ostian way on the spot, where, according to legend, the apostle had suffered, the church was enlarged by the Emperor Honorius, c. 404, and was spared by the Goths under Alaric. On July 17, 1823, the church was destroyed by fire, and after reconstruction was consecrated by Pius IX in 1854.

years of indulgences, and as many quarantines, and the remission of a third part of all sins ; on the feast of the dedication of the same church (which is within the octave of St. Martin), there are a thousand years of indulgences and as many quarantines, and the remission of a third part of all sins.

Also, if any one shall visit this same church on every Sunday in the year he shall have as great indulgences as he would have for crossing over to the Sepulchre of the Lord in Jerusalem, or to St. James in Spain (*Galicia*).

Also, in the same church repose a large part of the bodies of the Holy Innocents ; the arm of St. Anne the mother of Mary ; and the fetter with which St. Paul was shackled.

THE CHURCH OF ST. MARY THE GREATER[1]

The fourth church is the church of St. Mary the Greater.[1] In this church there are every day xlviii years of indulgences, and as many quarantines, and the remission of a third part of all sins.

The relics of the aforesaid church are these :* First, the body of St. Matthew the apostle, which lieth beneath the high altar ; the body of St. Jerome ; the bodies of SS. Romula and Redempta ; the mantle of the Blessed Virgin Mary in which her Son reposed in the manger ; the cradle of Christ ; the stole of St. Jerome ; the arm of St. Thomas of Canterbury.

Also, on the ninth day of the month of May there is remission of all sins, which was given by Pope Pius the second. Here too, on all feasts of the Blessed Virgin Mary, a thousand years of indulgences are bestowed ; and from the feast of the assumption of Mary the Virgin to her Nativity a thousand years of indulgences.

[1]Founded by Pope Liberius (352-356), rebuilt by Sixtus III (432-440) it was probably the first Roman church dedicated to the Virgin Mary.
*Fo. 7a.

c

THE CHURCH OF ST. LAURENCE[1]

The fifth church is the church of St. Laurence[1]. In this church there are certain indulgences granted by St. Silvester, the Pope, and by St. Pelagius, who consecrated the same church, namely, on every day xlviii years of indulgences, and as many quarantines, and the remission of a third part of all sins.

Here too is the stone on which St. Laurence was placed after his death by roasting.

If any one shall visit the said church on every Wednesday during a whole year, he shall be permitted to free one soul from purgatory.

Also, on the feasts of SS. Stephen and Laurence, whose bodies rest beneath the high altar, there are lxxx years of indulgences and as many quarantines, and the remission of a third part of all sins[2].

THE CHURCH OF ST. SEBASTIAN[3]

The sixth church is the church of St. Sebastian. In this church, there are every day xlviii years of indulgences, and as many quarantines, and the remission of a third part of all sins.

Also, in the same church there are every day a thousand years of indulgences, and as many quarantines, and the remission of a third part of all sins,— these were given by Pope Pelagius.

The indulgences in this church are as great as those obtainable in the churches of the apostles Peter and

[1]The basilica of St. Laurence, outside the walls, according to legend was built by Constantine on the Tiburtine way, it was enlarged by Pope Pelagius II (578-590) and again by Honorius III in 1216.

[2]To the above five basilican churches two others were added in the sixth century, viz. : St. Sebastian on the Appian Way and St. Cross *in Jerusalem*.

[3]Fo. 7b. 'The erection of this basilica—on the Appian Way—is attributed to Constantine. It was remodelled by Cardinal Scipio Borghere in 1611.

Paul, because for about lxx years their bodies lay hid here. Also, Popes Silvester, Gregory, Alexander, and Nicholas granted, each one after the other, a thousand years of indulgences to all persons who shall visit this church for worship, prayer, or pilgrimage, at any time of the year. In the said church rest the bodies of xviii martyred popes each one of whom giveth his own indulgence. And many other indulgences there are in the aforesaid church which cannot be enumerated, because the bodies that rest there are countless.

Also, in the cemetery of Kalixtus there is plenary remission of all sins.

Also, in the same church there is—as one reads in Roman history (*Romanis historiis*)—one Sunday in the month of May on which all sins are . . . (*a word or two obliterated*).

THE CHURCH OF THE HOLY CROSS[1]

The seventh church[2] is the church of the Holy Cross. In this church there are on every day xlviii years of indulgences, and the remission of a third part of all sins.

Also, under the high altar rest the bodies of the martyrs, Anastasius and Casius.

Constantana (*sic*), the daughter of Constantine, built this church in honour of the Holy Cross at the request of St. Helen, and Pope Silvester consecrated it. Here, on all Sundays in the year there are cccliii years of indulgences, and as many quarantines, and the remission of a third part of all sins.

In the aforesaid church there are these relics :—
Two sapphires, one of which is filled with the blood

[1]Fo. 8a. [2]The Liber Pontificalis ascribes this church to the Empress Helena, mother of Constantine. It was repaired by Gregory II in 720, and again by Lucius II (1144-1145). Much of its primitive basilican form was destroyed by Benedict XIV. c. 1774.

[2]S. Croce in Gerusalemme.

of Christ, and the other with the milk of the Blessed Virgin Mary ; the sponge in which they offered the vinegar and salt to Christ on the Cross ; xi thorns from the crown of Christ.

Within the high (*maius*) altar, is the wood of the holy cross of the penitent thief who was crucified with Christ. In the chapel which is called the Jerusalem chapel, into which women do not enter, there is plenary remission of all sins.

Having spoken of the indulgences of the principal churches, it remains to say something concerning the other churches of minor importance. (*rubricated*)*

In connexion with the towers, and springs (*fontibus*) there are every day seven thousand (years) of indulgences, and it has been proved by those who have made the experiment that whensoever anyone drinketh of the three springs he shall be freed at once from any infirmity that may affect him.

In the church of ST. MARY OF THE HEAVENLY ALTAR[1] there are a thousand years of indulgences and as many quarantines, and the remission of a third part of all sins ; and on the day of the Annunciation of Mary, the Holy Virgin, full remission of all sins.

There is a picture here of the Blessed Virgin Mary painted by St. Luke ; and the foot prints of the holy Angel.

Also, in the church of ST. MARY OF THE PEOPLE[2], there are two thousand years of indulgences.

Here, too, is a picture of the Blessed Virgin Mary painted by St. Luke.

Also in the church of ST. MARY THE NEW[3], there are CC (200) years of indulgences and the remission of a third part of all sins. Here, also, is a picture of the Blessed Virgin Mary painted by St. Luke.

*Fo. 8b.
[1]S. Maria in Ara Cœli.
[2]Fo. 9a.   S. Maria del Popolo.
[3]S. Maria Nuova.

Also, in the church of ST. MARY, over the Bridge are pillars (*statua*) at which St. Peter and blessed Paul were martyred, here, there are a thousand years of indulgences.

Also, in the church of ST. MARY THE ROUND[1], there is remission of a third part of all sins ; and on all Saints' Day, and on the ninth day of May, there is true remission of all sin.

Also, in the church of ST. PETER'S CHAINS[2], is the chain with which St. Peter was bound—which Constantana (*sic*), the daughter of the Emperor, brought from Jerusalem. There is remission of all sins on the first day of the month of August.

Also, in the church of ST. JOHN BEFORE THE LATIN GATE[3], where St. John was boiled (*coctus*) in oil, one soul can be freed from purgatory.

Also, in the church of ST. SILVESTER,[4] is the head of St. John the Baptist, here, there are a thousand years of indulgences.

Also, in the church of ST. JAMES, is the stone on which our Lord Jesus Christ was circumcised in Solomon's Temple. Here, there are five hundred years of indulgences.

Also, in the church of ST. PRASSEDE[5], there is a third part of the pillar (*statua*) at which our Lord Jesus Christ was scourged. Here are three thousand years of indulgences.

Also, in the church of ST. BARTHOLOMEW[6], the

[1]S. Maria Rotonda, or St. Maria ad Martyres another name for the Pantheon.

[2]S. Pietro in vincoli, upon the Esquiline, the church is said to have been founded by Eudoxia, daughter of Theodosius and wife of Valentinian III.

[3]S. Giovanni a Porta Latina was built by Pope Gelasius (492-496) and rebuilt in 772 and 1151.

[4]S. Silvestro. [1]In the Piazza S. Silvestro, the church was built by Paul I (757-767) and rebuilt by Innocent III (1198-1216).

[5]S. Prassede. The church is said to have been built on the site of the house of Prassede daughter of Pudens a contemporary of St. Peter. It was rebuilt by Paschal I (871-824), and many of its ancient features were destroyed in the XVIth century by St. Charles Borromeo.

[6]S. Bartolomeo All' Isola.

saint himself lieth beneath the high altar, and St. Paulinus with him. Here there are two thousand years of indulgences, and as many lents.

Also, in the HOLY FIELD (*Campo Santo*) there are every day, fifteen hundred years of indulgences.

Also at Rome the indulgences are doubled during all Lent and at the Ember seasons. (*rubricated*).

It is stated in the guide-books (*historiis*) that the pillar where Jesus Christ was bound shows marks of blood[1], etc. See the account of the dedication of the church.

CONCERNING WHAT IS FOUND IN THE MOLON (*molono*)[2] OF ST. PETER.

It is recorded in ecclesiastical history, and it is to be found in the Molon of St. Peter, or in a book such as that which blessed Gregory, the venerable doctor, ordered to be compiled, that in all the churches of Rome Stations should be made for the remission of sins every day during Lent, and to all persons, who (being confessed and truly contrite), shall visit the place named on the day of the Station indulgences were granted by the said Gregory.

The aforesaid processions (*circuli*) to all the churches, chapels, and oratories of the fair city of Rome have been approved, ratified, and confirmed by successive chief pontiffs. Moreover, lest the seed of ancient error should sprout from the images of demons, the same Gregory generally caused their heads and limbs to be hacked off, and by so doing he extirpated the deceptive root, and caused the palm of ecclesiastical truth to flourish more abundantly.

[1] " Credo in illa parte que iam Jerusalem dicitur " is written in the margin at the foot of the page.

[2] Fo. 10a.   *Molonus*, according to Ducange, is derived from a Spanish word meaning a heap, as *congeries garbarum*. I can only suggest that possibly the Molon of St. Peter was a book containing *miscellaneous* matter.

On the first day of the week for all who come devoutly for pilgrimage or prayer to the church of blessed Peter, there are three years (of indulgence), and he (St. Gregory), in his mercy, relaxed the penance enjoined for forgotten sins, and broken vows, provided there be no return to the said sins.

Also, at the end of each Station the years or days of the indulgences are reckoned in addition to the indulgences of the whole Station, according to the grant of the said blessed Gregory, which also was approved, ratified, and confirmed, by his successors.

On Septuagesima Sunday at St. Laurence without the walls, 1 year xl days.

On Sexagesima Sunday at St. Paul's, 1 year xl days.

THE STATIONS OF ROME[1]

On Quinquagesima Sunday at St. Peter's 1 year xl days.

On the fourth day of the week, that is to say Ash Wednesday, at the beginning of the fast, at St. Sabina, xl days.

On the fifth day of the week at SS. George and Alexis, xl days.

On the sixth day of the week at SS. John and Paul, xl days.

On the same day at St. Lucy, *In Septem Soliis*, 1 year xl days.

On Saturday at St. Tripho xl days.

On the first Sunday of Lent at St. John Lateran 1 year xl days.

On the second day of the week at St. Peter's Chains xl days.

On the same day at St. Blaise 1 year xl days.

[1]Fo. 10b. Johannes Fronto in *Praenotatis ad Kalend' Rom'* says : Statio non erat aliud quam confluxus cleri et populi præsente episcopo in locum ubi illo die publica missarum solemnia fieri debebant.

On the fourth day of the week at St. Mary the Greater 1 year xl days.

On the third day of the week at St. Anastasia xl days.

On the fifth day of the week at St. Laurence in Panisperna xl days.

On the sixth day at the Holy Apostles xl days.

On Saturday at St. Peter's 1 year xl days.

On the second Sunday in Lent at St. Mary in Dominica xl days.

On the second day of the week at St. Clement's xl days.

On the third day of the week at St. Balbina xl days.

On the fourth day of the week at St. Cecilia xl days.

On the fifth day of the week at St. Mary on the other side of the Tiber xl days.

On the sixth day of the week at St. Vitalis xl days.

On the same day at St. Andrew xl days.

On the Saturday at SS. Marcellin and Peter, xl days.

On the third Sunday in Lent at St. Laurence outside the walls 1 year xl days.*

On the second week-day at St. Mark, the evangelist, xl days.

On the same day at SS. Fabian and Sebastian iii years xl days.

Also at St. Anastasius 1 year xl days.

On the third day of the week at St. Potenciana xl days.

On the same day at St. Laurence in Panisperna 1 year xl days.

On the fourth day of the week at St. Sixtus xl days.

On the same day at "Lord whither goest Thou" (*domine quo vadis*).

On the fifth day of the week at SS. Cosmas and Damian iii years xl days.

On the sixth day of the week at St. Laurence in Lucina xl days.

*Fo. 11a.

On the same day at St. Mary in the Gate 1 year
xl days.

On the Saturday at St. Susanna in Lucina xl days.

On the fourth Sunday of Lent, at the Holy Cross of
Jerusalem 1 year xl days.

On the second day of the week at the Four Crowned
Saints xl days.

On the third day of the week at St. Laurence in
Damaso xl days.

Also at St. Maria in Grotta Pincta xl days.

On the fourth day of the week at St. Paul 1 year
xl days.

On the fifth day at St. Martin in Montibus xl days.

On the sixth day of the week at St. Eusebius xl days.

On the same day at St. Viviana 1 year xl days.

On Saturday at St. Nicholas in Carceribus xl days.

On the fifth Sunday in Lent at St. Peter's a year and
xl days.*

On the same day at St. James in Portica 1 year xl
days.

On the second day of the week at St. Crisogonus
xl days.

On the same day at St. Magdalena in Insula 1 year
xl days.

On the third day of the week at St. Ciriac xl days.

On the fourth day of the week at St. Marcellus xl
days.

On the same day at the Holy Apostles two quarantines.

On the fifth day of the week, at St. Apollinaris xl
days.

On the same day, at St. Benedict in Termis xl days.

On the sixth day of the week at St. Stephen's in
Celio Monte xl days.

On the same day at the Holy Hospital of St. Matthew
1 year xl days.

*Fo. 11b.

On Saturday at St. John Ante Portam Latinam xl days.

On the same day at St. John Lateran, 1 year and xl days.

Also in the Chapel where St. John was boiled (*coctus*) xl days.

On the sixth Sunday in Lent at St. John Lateran a year and xl days.

On the second day of the week at SS. Nereus and Achileus xl days.

On the same day at St. Gregory 1 year xl days.

Also at St. Anastasia 1 year xl days.

On the third day of the week at St. Prisca xl days.

On the same day at St. Aleuum (? *S. Aleaume*) three lents.

On the third day of the week at St. Mary Major 1 year xl days.

On the same day at St. Adrian 1 year xl days.

On the fifth day of the week at St. John Lateran 1 year xl days.

On the same day absolution to all true penitents is wont to be given by the Lord Pope or by a Cardinal.

On the sixth day of the week at the Jerusalem chapel a year xl days.*

On the same day at St. Mary in the Greek School[1] 1 year xl days.

On Saturday there is no Station but one goes to St. John Lateran, xl days.

Also at St. James below the Aventine hill 1 year xl days.

On Easter Sunday at St. Mary Major a year and xl days.

On the second day of the week at St. Peter 1 year xl days.

*Fo. 12a.

[1]Afterwards known as S. Maria in Cosmedin, "ubi Scs Thomas Cantuariensis tenuit scholas," *Liber Indulgentiarum*, R. 55. Vat. Cod.

On the third day of the week at St. Paul 1 year xl days.

On the fourth day of the week at St. Laurence outside the walls, 1 year xl days.

On the fifth day of the week at the Holy Apostles xl days.

On the sixth day of the week at St. Mary Round xl days.

On the Sunday within the octave of Easter at St. Pancras xl days.

On the greater Litany days, a Station at St. Peter 1 year xl days.

On the feast of the Ascension of the Lord at the (Church of the) Holy Apostles 1 year xl days.

On the Feast of Pentecost at St. Peter a year and xl days.

On the second day of the week at St. Peter Ad Vincula xl days.

On the third day of the week at St. Anastasia xl days.

On the fifth (*sic*) day of the week there is no Station here but at St. Laurence there are xl days.

On Saturday at St. Peter 1 year xl days.

On the first Sunday in Advent at St. Mary Major a year and xl days.

On the second Sunday in Advent at Holy Cross a year and xl days.

On the third Sunday in Advent at St. Peter's 1 year and xl days.

On the fourth day of the week during Embertide in Advent, at St. Mary Major 1 year xl days.*

On the sixth day of the week at the Holy Apostles xl days.

On Saturday at St. Peter 1 year and xl days.

On the fourth Sunday, at the Holy Apostles xl days.

On the fourth day of the week during the Ember season of the month of September, there is a Station at St. Mary Major, a year and xl days.

*Fo. 12b.

On the sixth day of the week at the Holy Apostles xl days.

On Saturday at St. Peter 1 year xl days.

On the fourth Sunday at the Holy Apostles xl days.

On the fourth day of the week in Ember week in the month of September, there is always a Station at St. Mary Major 1 year xl days.

At the sixth day of the week at the Holy Apostles xl days.

On the day of St. Peter's chair, there is always a Station at St. Bunana (*sic*) (? *Bibiana*) three years xl days and xl days, and this indulgence lasts for eight days.

On the feast of blessed Gregory, in the basilica of St. Peter, three years and xl days.

On the same day in the chapel of St. Gregory, near the steps of St. Peter 1 year xl days.

Also at St. Gregory in Septem Soliis 1 year xl days.

On the day of the Annunciation of Blessed Mary at St. Peter's, 1 year xl days.

On the same day at St. Mary Major 1 year xl days.

On the same day at St. Mary of the Annunciation, there is plenary remission.

FEASTS OF THE PALACE OBSERVABLE IN THE ROMAN COURTS* (*rubricated*).

From the Feast of the Circumcision of the Lord to the morrow of the Lord's Epiphany ; the feasts of St. Anthony the Abbot xvii (Jan.) ; of SS. Fabian and Sebastian xx (Jan.) ; of St. Agnes the virgin xxi (Jan.) ; of St. Vicent xxii (Jan.) ; of the Conversion of St. Paul xxv (Jan.) ; of the Purification of Blessed Mary ii (Febr.) ; of St. Blaise iii (Feb.).

*Fo. 13a.

ST. PETER IN CARCERE.

In this present church of St. Peter in Prison, is remission of a third part of all sins, and, two hundred years of indulgences on every day. These indulgences were granted by the chief pontiffs to all persons who, being truly penitent, and confessed, shall visit the aforesaid church for worship, or pilgrimage, or shall have bestowed alms in their own churches.

And here, lower down (*inferius*), is the spring which miraculously appeared when St. Peter baptized St. Process and St. Martinian, the warders of the said prison.

He who passes along this way should always say an *Ave Maria*. This chapel[1] is the second in all the world which was founded in honour of the Blessed Virgin Mary and is called the Heavenly Stairway (*Scala celi*),* upon which Blessed Bernard was deemed worthy to behold the ladder which reached up to heaven.

Whosoever shall celebrate in this chapel, or shall cause another so to do, for the souls that are in purgatory, they (*the said souls*) shall be set free at once for the merits of the Blessed Virgin Mary, and whatsoever petition is devoutly made here shall certainly be granted. In this place also there are many indulgences as is set forth more fully in the table of indulgences.

Here too are laid up the glorious bones of ten thousand martyrs.

In Rome there is an inscription saying : (*rubricated*) " This is the cemetery of St. Kalixtus, pope, and martyr, whosoever shall enter it, confessed, and contrite, shall have remission of all his sins."

At a certain spot where the saints rest, is the following inscription : " The body of St. Sebastian

[1] S. Maria della Scala.
*Fo. 13b.

lieth under the lower (*inferius*) altar, where St. Gregory, the pope, as he was celebrating, saw God's angel which said to him as he was occupied in the solemnities of the mass : ' This is a most holy place, in which is the true promise and unending joy, all which Sebastian, Christ's Martyr, earned.' " Moreover there is a pious belief that whosoever shall devoutly celebrate at this altar, or shall cause such celebration to be made there, shall free a soul from the pains of Purgatory.

Also, near the said altar, where there is an iron cross, resteth the body of Lucina, virgin[1] who buried the body of the said blessed Sebastian in the said place, and built the church to the honour of the same Sebastian.

Whosoever shall say daily the psalm of the Blessed Mary, that is to say " *Magnificat* " shall on each occasion have xxxiii years xxxiii weeks and three days of indulgence[1].

THE CHURCH OF ST. JOHN LATERAN, THE HEAD OF THE WORLD AND OF THE CITY*

[After a blank space the following Indulgence of Pope Gregory XI, dated at Avignon, 9 May, 1377, is inserted, granting to the faithful who shall visit the church of St. John Lateran when the heads of SS. Peter and Paul are shown, a pardon as great as that given in the church of St. Peter when the *Veronica* is shown].

Gregorius episcopus servus servorum Dei per perpetuam rei memoriam prerogativa speciali favoris & gracie ecclesie Lateratensium, que super omnes urbis & orbis supremum locum obtinere noscitur, presentes delectantes ac cupientes ut ecclesia ipsa in qua apostolorum Petri & Pauli capita venerabiliter requiescunt congruis honoribus frequentetur, & ut Christi fideles conlibencius causa devocionis confluant ad eandem, quo ibidem uber ius dono celestie gracie conspicerent, se esse refactos de omnipotentis Dei

[1]Lucina is generally described as a Matron.
*Fo. 14a.

misericordia, & dictorum apostolorum Petri & Pauli auctoritate confisi, auctoritate apostolica tenore presencium concedimus, ut omnes vere penitentes & confessi, qui dum huiusmodi capita ostendentur presentes erunt, tantam suorum peccaminum veniam consequantur, quantam consequentur vere penitentes & confessi qui in ostensione Veronice sunt presentes.* Nulli igitur homini liceat hanc paginam nostre concessionis infringere vel eam ausu temerario contraiere (*sic*). Si quis ac hoc attemptare presumpserit indignacionem omnipotentis Dei et beatorum apostolorum eius Petri & Pauli se noverit incursurum. Datum Auinion Septimo Idus Maii pontificatus nostri anno predicto.

AT THE HIGH ALTAR.

Also at the high altar of the said church of St. John Lateran there are indulgences of xlviii years and as many quarantines and the remission of a third part of all sins. Also, the emperor Constantine, after he had been cleansed from leprosy by receiving holy baptism, said to the blessed Silvester : " Behold, father, I have ordained that my house shall be God's church, bestow upon it thy bounteous blessing, and on all who shall enter therein." And to him the blessed Silvester said : " May the Lord Jesus Christ who cleansed thee from leprosy and purified thee in the never failing font, in his mercy, cleanse and purify all those who being free from mortal sin, shall come here, and by the authority of the apostles Peter and Paul and our's, let there be to them remission of all sins at any time of the year[1]."

*Fo. 15a.

[1]Fo. 15b.   The legendary baptism of Constantine by Pope Silvester in the Lateran church though lacking historical foundation, has found its way into the *Liber Pontificalis*.
Indulgentiae plenariæ quae a S. Silvestro concessisse dicuntur visitantibus ecclesiam Lateranensem nullum apud eruditos fidem merentur. Van Espen *op cit*. Vol. II, p. 230.

Also, St. Gregory, the pope, who consecrated this church after its destruction by heretics confirmed the indulgence which the aforesaid blessed Silvester, the pope, had ordained. Also, Pope Boniface VIII declared, " the indulgences of the Lateran church can be counted only by God," and, " all these indulgences I confirm."

Also, on the feast of the Holy Saviour whose picture miraculously appeared to all the Roman people, that is to say to all those who were there assembled when Pope Silvester consecrated the said church. Moreover, the picture remained visible on the wall, and can be seen there daily ; nor could the fire consume it when, on two occasions, the church was burnt[1].

Sure remission of all sins (*is given here*).

Also, Pope Boniface declared : " If any person shall come to our Lateran throne (*sedem*) for devotion, prayer, or pilgrimage, he shall be cleansed from all stain of sin.

Also, in the aforesaid church, in the chapel of St. John the Baptist, into which women do not enter, at the fountains (*fontes*) there is remission of all sins.

Also, in the chapel of St. Laurence, into which women do not come, and which is called the Holy of Holies, there is remission of all sins.

[1]The Lateran Church according to tradition was built by Constantine. It was completely rebuilt by Pope Sergius III (904-911), and was almost totally destroyed by fire in 1308. It was rebuilt by Clement V and his successor John XXII, but was again burnt in 1360. During the pontificate of Innocent X (1644-1655) the church was rebuilt for the third time and has been subjected to further alterations in 1732 and 1878.

The mosaic portrait of Christ in the oratory of St. Venance in the apse of St. John Lateran, is of great antiquity. Dom H. Leclercq is of opinion that it may possibly date from the time of Constantine, or have been executed after the pillage of Rome by Genseric in 455. It was restored by Pope Nicholas IV, in 1290, who added an inscription, stating that he had put back the Holy Face where it first *miraculously* appeared when the church was consecrated. It would appear, however, that in the eleventh century the superhuman origin of the picture was not recognised, since it is described in a document of that period as " imago Salvatoris depicta parietibus primum *visibiliter* omni populo apparuit," and that later *miraculose* was substituted for *visibiliter*. See *Dictionaire d'Archéologie Chrétienne*. Art. Latran. Details of the mosaic are reproduced by Marucchi in his Elements D'Archeologie Cretienne p. 96.

Also, if people only knew how great are the indulgences of the Lateran church, they would not think it necessary to go across the sea to the Holy Sepulchre.

THE TABERNACLE OF THE RELICS.

Also, in the nearest tabernacle (? *to the altar*) are these relics :—

The tiara or coronet (*regnum*) with which St. Silvester, the pope, was crowned[1].

Also, the head of St. Zachary, the father of St. John the Baptist.

Also, the head of St. Pancras, which dripped with blood for three days, when this church was burnt by the heretics.

(Here are) certain relics of St. Mary Magdalen.

The knife of St. Laurence, the martyr.

A tooth of the apostle Peter.

The cup in which St. John the Evangelist drank the poison, and received no hurt.

The chain (*cathena*) with which St. John the Evangelist was bound when he was led from Ephesus to Rome.

The tunic of St. John the Evangelist*, which was placed over three dead persons and forthwith they arose[2].

The ashes of St. John the Baptist, and some of his hair.

Some of the milk, hair, and vestments of St. Mary

---

[1]The tiara which Silvester received from Constantine was taken to Avignon, but was restored to the Lateran church by Eugenius IV, whence it was stolen in the time of Innocent VIII (1484-1492)—not long after Brewyn wrote. See Rospone *De Basilica Lateranensis*, quoted by Nichols in his translation of *Mirabilia*, p. 124.

*Fo. 16b.

[2]The legend of the resuscitation of three young men who had died from drinking poison, occurs in *De rebus a S. Johanne Evangetista gestis*—C.XX. Fabricius, *Codex Apocryphus Novi Testamenti* p. 575.

the Virgin, and the shirt which the Virgin Mary made with her own hands, for Jesus Christ.

The linen cloth with which Christ dried the feet of the Apostles at supper.

The pincers (*forbices*), and the reed with which Christ was smitten, and some of the wood of the cross.

The purple robe stained with drops of the blood of Christ.

The veil of the Blessed Virgin Mary, which she placed as drawers for Christ on the cross.

The foreskin of our Lord Jesus Christ when he was circumcised.

Some of the water and blood which flowed from the side of Christ.

In the greater tabernacle are the heads of the holy Apostles Peter and Paul, reverently laid up in a case of silver shaped like a man's head[1].

Also, in the chapel which is in the lower part of the church, over (*super*) the altar, is the table on which the Lord Jesus Christ supped with his disciples.

Also, the ark of the covenant, and Aaron's rod[2].

THE CHAPELS AT THE FONT OF CONSTANTINE.   Fo. 17a.

At the door where the Font (*fons*) of Constantine is, there hangs a tablet on which is the following inscription : " This church is called ' *Ad Fontes Constantini* ' because within this great circular building the Emperor Constantine was baptized by blessed Silvester, and Christ appeared to the said Constantine when he was baptized[3]."

In this church are many relics and many bodies of

[1]The heads of SS. Peter and Paul were removed from the Sancta Sanctorum by Urban V in 1367, and placed in silver busts near the high altar of the Lateran Church. The busts were destroyed by the French republicans. The present busts are copies made in 1804.

[2]On the margin at the foot of the page is written : " quasi valde . . . in almariolo nigro ferro incluso Anglice a cupbord."

[3]Montfaucon in his *Diarium Italicum*, p 136, says : " Baptisterium Constantini octangulum in quo putant baptizatium fuisse Constantinum magnum, *refragantibus* licet Eusebio, Athanasio, etc."

Saints and many indulgences, and especially in the chapel of St. John the Baptist[1], into which women do not enter, where there is remission of all sins ; and it (*the chapel*) is called an appendage (*appendix*), because it depends on the Lateran church, in which (chapel) there are infinite indulgences and remission of all sins. In the chapel which is on the other side of this circular building, or baptistry, and is called the chapel of St. Venance, the martyr, are the bodies of ten saints, to wit, Venance, Dominus, Anastasius, Maurus, Asterius, Septimitelius, Antiochialis, Paulus, Manus and Gaianus, together with many other relics.

Also, in this chapel there is a picture (*imago*) of the Blessed Virgin Mary which has worked many miracles. Another chapel, which is on the right hand side, is that of the holy virgins and martyrs, Ruffina and Secunda, and within it are their bodies.

Another chapel, which is on the left hand side and extends as far as the door, is that of blessed John, in which St. Gregory often used to pray, and in it are many indulgences.

In a chapel which is outside in the court, where the alabaster columns are, there are infinite indulgences, and, in it is the study of blessed Gregory, the whole[2] of which was adorned with mosaic work.

THE RELICS IN THE CHAPEL OF THE SAVIOUR[3].

In the chapel of the Saviour, or, as it was called in

[1]Pope Hilary, 461-468, built on either side of the baptistery of Constantine two chapels ; the one dedicated to St. John the Baptist and the other to St. John the Evangelist. Dom. H. Le Clercq *at supra*.

[2]The oratory of St. Venance on the south side of the baptistry of Constantine was built by Pope John IV (640-642).

[3]The oratory of St. Laurence, called later " *Sancta Sanctorum* " appears for the first time under Pelagius I (555-559), but the date of its foundation is unknown. It was rebuilt, or restored, in the XIIIth cent. A catalogue of the relics in the Sancta Sanctorum was compiled by a certain deacon named John in the XIIIth century and is printed in Mabillon's *Musaeum Italicum*, Vol. II, p. 572.

old time, of St. Laurence,—in the holy Lateran palace, there is a picture of the Saviour by St. Luke, but he did not put in the colours (*non imposuit colores*), as is plain from the following inscription : . . . (*the inscription is not given*). Very precious treasures (*pignora*) are contained here, as well of the Lord Saviour Himself— (whose praiseworthy picture here shineth forth),—as of the blessed apostles, martyrs, confessors and virgins, nearly all of which are laid up in a certain cypress chest, which Leo the third (795-816) ordered to be made, but Kalixtus, the second (1119-1124), placed the chest containing these divine treasures, which was formerly outside, within the altar of the blessed Laurence.

Now in this chapel there are three coffers ; in the one which is in the form of a cross, there is a cross of the purest gold, adorned with jacinths, smaragds and prasins, and in the middle of this cross is a piece cut from the umbelical cord of our Lord Jesus Christ ; the foreskin of the circumcision of Jesus Christ was in this holy place, but the chief pontiff adorned therewith the basilica of Constantine, and it is shown every year on the Sunday of the Lord's Resurrection immediately after dinner*.

This cross is anointed every year with sweet oil (*balsamo*) when the lord Pope, on the day of the exaltation of the Holy Cross, goeth in procession with the Cardinals from his palace into the said basilica of Constantine.

The other silver coffer contains a golden cross inlaid (*variata*) with electron, within which is a cross made of the very wood of the Cross on which the Saviour of the world hung. In another silver coffer are the sandals which are the very shoes which the Lord Jesus wore.

There is also another gilded coffer in which is a large piece of the wood of the same cross, which

*Fo. 18a.

Eraclius, the Persian[1], brought here, together with the body of St. Anastasius; it is now under the aforesaid altar.

Here also is one loaf of the Lord's Supper, and twelve of the lentils of the same Supper.

Some of the reed which smote the head of Jesus.

Some of the sponge, which, full of vinegar, they put to the mouth of Jesus.

Some of the wood of the sycomore tree up which Zacchaeus climbed.

Also, at one time, the heads of the Apostles Peter and Paul were here, but the blessed Pope Urban the fourth (1261-1264) removed them and set them up, marvellously adorned, over the high altar of the Lateran church, in the presence of all the people of Rome; but the other relics aforesaid, he suffered to remain in this same chapel.[1]

[Other relics are]:

The chin of the Apostle St. Bartholomew*.

The relics of St. Matthew, the Evangelist,—in a crystal phial.

Some of the garment of blessed John, the Evangelist—in a silver coffer.

The relics of St. John the Baptist,—in an ebony coffer.

Coals sprinkled with the blood, or fat, of the blessed Laurence.

The arm of St. Cesar.

The relics of St. Stephen, the pope.

The knife of the blessed Denys, the Areopagite.

[The relics] of St. Sebastian; of St. Tiburce, the son of Chomancius (*sic*) (*Chromacius*); of the seven holy brethren; of SS. Nereus and Achilles; of Aquila and

---

[1]Heraclius, Emperor of the East, 610-641, distinguished himself in the wars against the Persians, and recovered the true Cross which in the earlier years of his reign had fallen into the hands of the Persians.

*Fo. 18b.

Prisca ; of Abdon and Senne ; of Processus and
Martian ; of Mark and Marcellian ; of Primus and
Felician ; of Felix and Adaucte ; of Erene and Abande ;
of Pigmenius (*Pigmene*), Sisinius, and Sacraninus ;
(? *Saturninus*).

The relics of the Confessors, Damasus (*sic*) the pope ;
Felix, the pope ; Poncianus, the pope ; Jerome and
Felix, priests ; the head of St. Praxedes ; the head of St.
Barbara.

The relics of SS. Anastasia, Eulalia, Agape, Cionia,
Hereneas, Pista and Cipisa.

The heads of the holy virgin martyrs Agnes, and
Euphemia ; and the head of St. Agnes which still
retains its very beautiful hair[1].

In the same oratory also, are the relics of the
following saints, namely, of the forty holy martyrs
and of many others. Note that at the foot of the said
picture of the Saviour, there is a row of stones from
the Holy Land ; a stone from holy Bethlehem ; part of
the manger in which Christ was laid ; some of the
place which is called " *licostratos*[2]."

Some of the pillar to which Christ was bound ; some
of the place called Calvary ; some of the wood of the
Lord's cross ; some of the spear with which the side
of Christ was pierced ; some of the Lord's sepulchre ;
some of the stone on which the Angel sat ; some of
Mount Sion ; some of Mount Sinai ; some of the
sepulchre of St. Mary, the mother of God.

Also, in the upper part of this most sacred altar are

[1]When the iron grille in front of the altar was opened in 1903 the head of
St. Agnes was discovered in a silver casket within the cyprus chest. On the
casket was an inscription, written in ink : Honorius P.P. III Fieri Fecit pro
capite Beate Agnetis. Dom Leclercq gives an illustration of the casket and
of the skull of the saint to which, however, no hair is attached ; but Nicholas
Signorelli in an inventory of the relics in the *Sancta Sanctorum* compiled in
the XIV cent. mentions the head of St. Agnes with some of the flesh and
hair. *Le Clercq Op. Cit. Art. Latran.*

[2]Lithostratos, i.e. The Pavement, in the Vulgate (St. John IX, 13) *sedit pro
tribunali in loco qui dicitur Lithostratos.*

two openings (*fenestrae*) having what appear to be iron doors, in one of which are the bodies of virgins, to wit, of the Holy Innocents, and in the other the bodies, or relics of holy martyrs and confessors.

* * *

It came to pass as a certain man* of very holy life, [A space is left here, and *Mirabilia* is written in the margin] was communing with the Lord by night, before the doors of this basilica, within the octave of the Assumption of Mary, two men of venerable appearance, placed themselves at his side, who clearly had not come from this world. When he asked wherefore they had come, they replied, " We are waiting for our Lady, who, as if in repayment to her Son for His journey, has been wafted hither with majesty to do Him respect, and because He by commanding her attendance at His coming, has done her great honour[1]. Therefore be thou neither fearful nor alarmed, for thine eyes shall see wondrous things." And lo ! suddenly there appeared a multitude of the souls now reigning with Christ, and a glorious host of holy spirits, which in choirs sang praise to the Lord in clear sweet tones, amongst whom a choir of holy women led the way, followed by the confessors, of various orders, next to whom marched the martyrs, followed by the Apostles, and last of all came the most glorious Mother of God, attended by choirs of angels, and diffusing a wondrous perfume. At her entrance an intense splendour shone forth like unto the lightning, so that the whole fabric (*machina*) of the palace seemed to be on fire, and its appearance utterly transformed. Spell-bound by the glorious vision, the man seemed to be on the point of collapse, but he was reassured by the two men at his side, who said, " Be not afraid for it is the majesty of the Lord which is

---

*Fo. 19a.

[1]The text is very obscure here, " expectamus que quasi iter rependens filio cum maiestate ventata est ut ei deferat, et quia ipse imperand' eam veniens grandem fecit ei honorem."

now approaching." Whereupon, comforted by their words, he raises his eyes and sees the glorious throne of the great God being carried up on high by the angels, but he saw no one sitting thereon. Presently the gates of the basilica were thrown open, and the heavenly throne is brought therein, also, the man who was deemed worthy to see this, is himself brought in together with others. In the meantime, the question is asked, " Who shall celebrate the divine mysteries ? " and answer is made, " The chief of the Apostles," and Laurence and Vincent shall act as his servers. At length when the solemn celebration was ended and all had departed, the chalice and paten were left upon the altar with the holy and divine things to testify to this stupendous vision, and in order that the assertion of the man who had seen it might receive full confirmation.

Further, concerning the chapel of the Saviour.

In the aforesaid chapel of the Saviour, there is an ancient picture of the Virgin Mary painted on a little square panel (*tabula*), but whether by blessed Luke, I do not know for certain ; however, so it was said. Also, in this chapel there is a lamp always burning.

Also, near the inner door there is painted upon the wall a very beautiful picture of the Virgin Mary.

Also, to the outer door there are gates of brass, and, hanging from a chain on the wall, is the slab (*mensa*) on which Jesus stood when He washed His disciples' feet.

Also, at some distance from this door, there is a column of white marble, which is said to have been miraculously split (*divisa*) by Jesus Christ, one part of which stands by the outer wall of the house or chapel, and the other part stands opposite to it by the wall on the other side of the same house.

Also, beyond this is a door of this same outer chapel, which faces towards Rome, the gates of which are of brass, and here are many steps of white marble, on one of which is the sign of the cross, with an iron grate placed over it.

Also, in this chapel are two or more chairs of red marble stone[1], with apertures carved in them, upon which chairs, as I heard, proof is made as to whether the pope is a male or not, etc[2].

Also, further on is a long building (*domus*) with many pictures of Blessed Mary and other saints.

Also, in the great house next to the church of St. John Lateran, where the Penitencers are wont to sit, there is a place at the end of the house where there are four marble columns and upon those four columns lieth a great broad stone, and it is said to be the measure of the height of Jesus Christ, beneath which pilgrims are wont to stand.

THE CHURCH OF ST. PETER*

In the church of St. Peter, concerning which many things have been related at the beginning of this book, after the description of the church of St. John Lateran, there are a number of columns of white marble marvellously carved to represent, as it were, vines with leaves and clusters of grapes, running up the pillars, beneath one of which, it is said, Jesus sat when He was preaching in Solomon's temple at Jerusalem, whence it was brought to Rome, and is now well protected with iron, and almost every day it works great virtues, especially on demented persons, and on those possessed by devils. A priest is often in attendance

---

[1] *Cathedrae de lapide marmoreo et rubio.*

[2] The story that the newly elected pope sat down on the pierced seat in order to give proof of his sex is first found in the Visions of the Dominican Robert D'Usez, (d. A.D. 1296), after him Jacobo D'Agnolo Di Scarpeia in the year 1405—describes the enthronisation of Gregory XII as an eyewitness, and adds that the supposed investigation is a senseless fable. Von Dollinger— *Fables respecting the Popes of the Middle Ages.*

*Fo. 21a.

with a book, who, vested in surplice and stole, is ready to help infirm folk by prayer, etc.

Also, there is in the church a great image of St. Peter[1] of cast metal.

Also, in the same church is the chair of St. Peter made of wood which is placed in a small chapel[2].

Also, at the door of the same church of St. Peter, towards the east, there is an image (*imago*) of St. Mary the Virgin, from which blood used to flow miraculously, the marks of which all persons who come here may plainly see on three stones which are laid on the ground, and, enclosed within a square grate, or fence of iron ; there is also a fourth stone—in the wall beneath the feet of the same image—without any ironwork. All the stones are of white marble[3].

*In the court before the door of St. Peter, stands the brasen pinnacle which was placed over the church of All Saints, otherwise called the Panteon[4], which, as it is said, the devil took up with the intention of casting, or hurling it up on the church of St. Peter the Apostle, that he might destroy it ; but by God's protecting grace, the church was uninjured, since the missile fell at some distance from it, almost in the middle of the court-yard, as may be seen to this day[5].

[1]Marucchi who gives an illustration of the statue in his *Elements d'Archeologie*, p. 129, is of opinion that the image may date from the Vth century, and was perhaps made by order of S. Leo V, after the defeat of Attila.

[2]Figured in Marucchi *op. cit* p. 127. Nothing appears to be known as to the origin of the chair.

[3]In the margin at the top of the page is written, "Prosam Sci Petri quere in parvo libra tuo.")

[4]The Pantheon was dedicated by Pope Boniface IV (c. A.D. 610) to the B.V.M. and all the martyrs. *Liber Pontificalis*, vita Bonifacii, and Paul the Deacon, *Hist. Langobardorum.*

[5]This must be the gilded bronze pine-cone which stood in the centre of the atrium at the West end of the Church. It served as a fountain and was placed there by Pope Damasus. It was popularly said to have come from the roof of the Pantheon, but really came from the summit of Hadrian's Mausoleum. See Tuker and Malleson's *Christian and Ecclesiastical Rome*, Pt. I. p.57.

*Fo. 21b.

Also, next the church is the chapel of St. Mary of
Fevers, in which persons suffering from that sickness,
are graciously cured by prayer, through the merits of
Mary, the mother of God.

Also, in the church of St. Peter, unless I am mis-
taken, is the head of St. James the Less, and of St.
Menne, the martyr. Now the middle doors are of cast
bronze curiously adorned with figures (*imaginibus*), and
I believe all the three doors are of bronze, etc[1].

Also, concerning the church of St. Peter in Carcere,
about which certain things have been noted above,
there is a picture of Processus and Martinianus, painted
over the baptistry door ; and here also are many steps
of white marble, about xxiiii, at the entrance of the
church.

Also, there are other steps at the entrance to the
well which was miraculously revealed.

The other remarkable things, and the relics, have
been mentioned above.

Also, in the church of St. Peter ad Vincula is the
chain with which St. Peter was bound.

PUDENCIANA[2]*

In the church of St. Potenciana (*sic*) there is a little
chapel in which St. Peter celebrated his first mass.

Also, in another and larger chapel in the same
church is laid up the blood of three thousand martyrs
in an aperture (*foramine*) which is walled round with
white marble arranged in a square ; and I have been
twice within it (*et fui interius bis*).

In this chapel is an altar near which is the mark
(*signum*) of the consecrated host, which fell upon a

[1]The bronze doors were the work of Florentine workers, and were
executed by order of Eugenius IV (1431-1447).

[2]The church of S. Pudentiana on the Viminal is said to have been built
during the second century on the site of the house in which the Senator
Pudems received St. Peter, and was restored during the pontificate of Siricius
(384-398) Gregorovius. op. cit.

*Fo. 22a.

stone of white marble imprinting it in a very miraculous manner ; this imprint is covered over with iron-work, " *Anglice* grated wt yren."

In this church also, is the bench upon which the Lord Jesus sat together with His disciples at the Supper ; also, some of the thorn and crown (*sic*) of the Lord, and part of one of the nails with which Christ was crucified, also some of the wood of the Cross of Christ.

Also, some of the stone of the Lord's tomb ; some of the stone of the pillar at which Christ was scourged in Jerusalem, in Pilate's house ; some of the crib in which Christ was born on the day of His Nativity ; some of the bones of St. Bartholomew the Apostle ; some of the ribs of St. James the Apostle ; a tooth of St. Peter the Apostle ; some of the garments, or priestly vestments of St. Andrew the Apostle ; some of the arm of St. Matthew, the Apostle and Evangelist ; a bone of St. Paul, the Apostle*.

Some of the head of St. Thomas, the Apostle ; a bone from the head of St. Barnabas, the Apostle ; some of the hairs of Mary Magdalene ; something of St. Potenciana ; some of the veil of the Virgin Mary ; some of the wood of the bier upon which the body of Mary was carried for burial.

Also, the relics of St. Silvester, St. Gregory, the Pope, Zachary, the prophet ; St. John the Baptist, etc.

This church is near to the church of St. Mary the Greater.

THE CHURCH OF ST. PAUL[1]

The church of St. Paul, the apostle, belongs to the monks of the order of St. Benedict.

*Fo. 22b.

[1]The basilica of St. Paul on the Ostian way, according to the Liber Pontificalis was erected by Constantine over the tomb of the Apostle. It was reconstructed on a larger scale by Valentinian II (386), and after being subjected to several restorations was almost completely destroyed by fire in 1823. The rebuilding of the church was completed in the year 1854.

Beneath the high altar are the glorious middle parts of the bodies of the holy apostles Peter and Paul, which a long time ago were divided by the blessed Pope Silvester.

On every day throughout the year, there are xlviii (years of) indulgences, as many quarantines, and the remission of a third part of all sins.

Also, on the feast of the holy Apostles Peter and Paul there are as many indulgences as there are at St. Peter's, namely, a thousand years.

Also, at the entrance of the same church, where the head of St. Paul was found, there are every day as many (*blank*) and also remission of a third part of all sins.

Also, on the feast of the Conversion of St. Paul, there are indulgences of a thousand years.

Also, on the day of the Holy Innocents,—many of whose bodies, together with those of blessed Timothy, Julian, and many other martyrs, rest in the same basilica,—there are indulgences of XL years.

Also, on the anniversary of the dedication of the same church that is to say, on the octave of St. Martin, there is remission of all sins.

Also, whosoever shall come to the said church on all Sundays during a whole year, shall have the indulgence which pilgrims who go to St. James of Spain (*Galiciae*) are said to have.

Also, in the said church is the chain with which St. Paul was bound ; an arm of St. Anne, the mother of Mary the Virgin with flesh on the bone (?) (*in carne ossis*) (sic) ; the head of St. Stephen, pope and martyr, and many other relics.

Also, to all and singular who shall give a helping hand to the building, or repair of the said church, the lord Martin (Martin V, 1417-1431) and the lord Eugenius, the fourth (1431-1447) granted and confirmed all the indulgences which aforetime had been granted by their predecessors in the office of chief pontiff[1].

St. Augustine saith : " Indulgence is given by divine grace and avails for the expiation of faults of ignorance, the blotting out of venial sins, the diminution of penance and for growth in grace[2]."

CONCERNING THE CROSS

Also, near the altar of St. Paul[3] is the picture (*imago*) of the crucifixion of the holy Saviour upon the Cross which spoke to St. Bridget[4], as she was praying, it is enclosed in ironwork.

At the west door of this church on the outside is an altar in which is an aperture, and here, as it is said, was found the head of St. Paul, etc.

The aforesaid church has many stone pillars of marble. The greater part of the ancient church was destroyed, I believe through lack of repair[5].

Also, on a tablet (*tabula*) in the church of St. Paul is the following inscription : *Bonum est nobis hic esse scilicet in claustro v in religionis statu*[6].

[1]Fo. 23b.

[2]In the Index to the great Paris Edition of St. Augustine's works I can find no reference to any passage corresponding to Brewyn's quotation.

[3]Church of St. Paul.

[4]St. Bridget of Sweden, canonised by Pope Boniface IX, A.D. 1391.

[5]In margin, *Sci Pauli in parvo libro.*

[6]In margin, *Utilitas religionis quare, quia homo viv⁺t purius, cadit rarius, surgit velocius, irroratur frequencius, incedit cautius, quiescit securius, purgatur cicius, morietur confidencius, et primiatur coposius, summa sapienta est cotidie de morte cogitare."*
[It is good for us to be here, that is to say in a cloister or religious (order). Wherefore ? Because a man liveth more chastely, falleth more rarely, riseth more quickly, is refreshed more frequently, walketh more warily, resteth more securely, is cleansed more speedily, will die more confidently, and will be rewarded more copiously. The highest wisdom is to meditate on death daily].

IN THE CHURCH OF ST. MARY
OF THE PEOPLE[1]*

This most holy basilica was built and consecrated to the honour of God Almighty, and the most Blessed Virgin Mary, by the Roman people ; and therefore is called St. Mary of the People ; and it is renowned for these holy and venerable sanctuaries :

In the first place, within the high altar, the venerable Pope Paschal, with ten cardinals, four bishops who were also archbishops, ten bishops, and many other prelates, consecrated the aforesaid altar, and laid up within it the relics which are described below, namely : a portion of the umbilical cord of our Lord Jesus Christ ; some of the milk, and a portion of the dress and head veil of the Virgin Mary.

These (*relics*) he enclosed in an ivory casket, and placed over them (*desuper*) some of the wood of the Cross ; they are all kept in a crystal vase (*ampulla*) within the said casket of ivory.

Also, some of the bones of the Apostles Peter and Paul are kept here ; some of the dust of the bones of St. John the Baptist ; some of the bones of St. Andrew, the Apostle ; some of the bones of St. Mary Magdalene, and of Pope Sixtus (119-128) the martyr ; something of SS. Rufina and Secunda, virgins ; something of St. Stephen, pope and martyr ; (Stephen I, 253-257) also of St. Stephen the protomartyr ; of St. Ypolitus† and his companions ; of St. Laurence the martyr ; of the xl martyrs ; of St. Agnes, virgin and martyr ; of St. Cecilia, virgin and martyr ; of St. Tiburcius, martyr ; of St. Urban, pope ; of St. Valerian, martyr ; and of many other saints whose names it would take a long time to relate.

*Fo. 24a. [1]An oratory was consecrated on the site of Nero's tomb by Paschal II (c. 1099) to dispel the evil spirits which were popularly supposed to haunt the spot. The church was built in 1227 at the cost of the people of Rome and was rebuilt by Sixtus IV, c. 1473.

†Fo. 24b.

On the day of the consecration of this altar, he
(*Pope Paschal*) granted a thousand years of indulgences,
and as many quarantines every day, in honour of the
glorious Virgin to all who shall come devoutly, and
give alms according to their ability, from the sixth
week day after the third Sunday in Lent to the octave
of Easter.

Also, on account of the personal presence of the
aforesaid Pope himself, and of the said cardinals, he
granted another thousand years, and as many quarantines, according to the numbers of the said cardinals,
that is, he reckoned a hundred years for each of them,
and as many quarantines.

Also, the aforesaid Pope granted xxxiii years and as
many quarantines, according to the number of the
other prelates, for each of whom he granted one year
and one quarantine.

Now the cause of the building and consecration of
this church, (*S. Maria Del Popolo*) according   to
what is contained in the privilege attached to the said
indulgences, was as follows :

In the time of the above-named Pope[1] where now
the high altar stands there was a certain nut-tree,—taller
than the other trees*,—in which the demons guarding
the body of Nero, used to hide[2], and these demons
were in the habit of killing by suffocation all who
passed through the Flaminian gate. Now when this
came to the ears of the said most holy pope Paschal,
he proclaimed a fast for all the people, while he himself,
together with the clergy, prayed steadfastly all night
that God, and the Blessed Virgin Mary, would
vouchsafe to release the people from such a horrible
and terrible plague (*peste*) ; and that God would be
pleased mercifully to reveal what should be done. On
the third night the Blessed Virgin appeared and spake

[1]Paschal II c. 1099.
*Fo. 25a.
[2]The legend of the haunted nut tree is to be found also in the Vatican
MS. m. 11—*Codex Monacens.*

to him in these words : " Paschal, go forth to the place which is called the Flaminian gate near to which you will find a nut-tree excelling in height the other trees, cause this tree to be cut down and entirely rooted up, and, on the same spot, cause a church to be built in my name." And after he (*the pope*), had awaked from sleep, he went to the aforesaid place, accompanied by a great concourse of people amongst, whom were clerks and prelates, and commanded that the said tree should be cut down and grubbed up from the roots. Now as soon as it was rooted up, every kind of demon fled away, and on the spot he (Paschal) with his own hands, built an altar, and afterwards, at its consecration, he rendered it illustrious, by bestowing upon it the above honourable relics and by granting the aforesaid indulgences.

THE INDULGENCES OF POPE GREGORY

Also, Gregory the ninth (1227-1241), out of reverence to the glorious Virgin* for the aforesaid miracle, lest the people of Rome should be ungrateful for so great a boon, and being anxious to induce them to pay more earnest devotion to the Virgin, came to the aforesaid church with many of the clergy, bringing with him a picture of the blessed Virgin, painted upon a panel (*tabula*) by the hand of Luke, the evangelist, and there, as he was celebrating the holy mysteries, he granted to all who shall come to the said church— being truly penitent and confessed—on all feasts of the Blessed Virgin Mary, and within the octave of the same, on the feast of the blessed Augustine, and within the octaves of the same, on the feasts of the Nativity, the Resurrection, the Ascension and Pentecost, and from the day of the church's consecration to the octaves of Easter, seven hundred years (*of indulgence*) and as many quarantines.

*Fo. 25b.

E

Also, the Vicar of the lord Pope Clement, the fourth (1265-1268), by mandate of the same, consecrated the altar of the blessed Mary Magdalene, on the second Sunday in the month of June, where, every year, he granted indulgence of vii years and as many quarantines to all who shall come devoutly and give alms, either on the day itself, or within its octave.

Also, the aforesaid vicar of the lord Pope Clement with many other bishops, by command of the same (*pope*), consecrated the altar of St. Augustine on the feast of the same venerable doctor, (Aug. 28) and granted to all persons who shall come devoutly on that day, and throughout its octave, seven years (of indulgence), and as many quarantines. And, for each one of the bishops, who were nine in number, he granted one quarantine.

In the last year of the pontificate of the lord Pope Boniface the eighth, (1303) and by his authority, the lord Patriarch of Constantinople* and the lord Archbishop of Bourges[1] with many other bishops, consecrated the altar of the blessed Katherine, virgin and martyr, and of St. Giles, the abbot, on the feast of the same Katherine, to which virgin the said pope was singularly devoted. At this hallowing the aforesaid patriarch and archbishop granted, by mandate of the lord pope, to all who shall come devoutly, and give alms, on the feast days of the aforesaid saints, forty years (*of indulgence*) and as many quarantines. All these indulgences the aforesaid Boniface granted to all who shall come truly penitent and confessed (making express mention concerning the things aforesaid), from the day of the consecration of that church until the octave of Easter, and praying to the Lady Mother of God that she may be always the advocate of the whole Christian world, and especially of the Roman people.

Also, the vicar of the lord Pope Clement the fourth

---

*Fo. 26a.   [1]In 1303 Leonardo Faliero was patriarch (latin) of Constantinople and Egidius de Colonna Archbishop of Bourges.

(1265-1268) granted indulgences—from the day of the consecration of the church to the octaves of Easter— of xvii years and as many quarantines.

The said indulgences amount in all to two thousand eight hundred and four years, and to two thousand one hundred and thirteen quarantines. Thanks be to God and Blessed Mary.

THE ALTAR OF HEAVEN (*ara celi*)[1]*

This is that venerable altar of Heaven concerning which in the lessons for our Lord's Nativity, we find these words :

" When the emperor Octavian had reduced the whole world to the rule of Rome, it pleased the Senate to will that he should be worshipped as God. The emperor, however, being a prudent man, and knowing that he was mortal, was unwilling to usurp to himself the attributes of deity (*deitatis nomen*). Nevertheless, at the pressing request of the Senate, he summoned the Sibylline prophetess, desiring to know by her oracular declaration, if any greater man than he had ever been born into the world. When therefore on the day of the Lord's Nativity, the Sybil being in the place which at that time was the Emperor's bed-chamber, there appeared at mid-day, a golden circle round the sun, and, in the midst of the circle, the most beautiful Virgin holding her Son in her arms. Then the Sybil showed the vision to the Emperor, who, as he was marvelling at this strange sight, heard a voice saying to him, ' This is the Heavenly Altar,' and forthwith he offered on this altar incense to the Christ and His Mother."

*Fo. 26b. [1]S. Maria in Ara Coeli, was called S. Maria in Capitolo until about the xivth century, according to Gregorovius (*Hist. of the City of Rome in the Middle Ages*, Trans. Hamilton. vol. IV, 45). The church in the middle ages became the centre of the parliamentary life of the Roman citizens.

Wherefore, that everything which is above written may be kept in remembrance, and all may know that this altar is the chief altar of the world, you will find, inscribed on marble, between two pillars, these verses :

Notatur versus (*rubricated*).

Luminis hanc almam matris qui scandis ad aulam
Cunctarum prima (*quae*)[1] fuit orbe sita ;
Noscas quod Cesar tunc construxit Octavianus
Hanc Aram celi sacra proles cum patet ei.

[Translation]

Know one and all who climb the heavenly stair
That this first altar of our Lady fair
By the Emperor Octavian was reared
What time to him the Holy Child appeared.

Afterwards Anacletus, the fourth pope* (76-90) after the blessed Peter, consecrated and dedicated this venerable Altar of Heaven. Within it lie the venerable bodies of these saints[2] :

Helen, the mother of the Emperor Constantine, who found the Cross of the Lord Jesus Christ ; the holy martyrs Arthemius, the tribune ; Abundus and Abundancius. The indulgence of this venerable altar of heaven (according to what is contained in the register of the lord Pope, which is kept in the registry of St. Peter in which all the indulgences of the city are registered) is three thousand years, and this is doubled on the feast of the Assumption, for then there are six thousand years, as I found inscribed on a tablet (*tabula*) upon (*super*) a sarcophagus, beneath the altar[3], which is called the altar of heaven.

Also, there is a picture of the Virgin Mary in the

[1]Quae omitted in text.

*Fo. 27a.

[2]The inscription is given by Gregorovius. *Op. cit.* vol. IV, p. 472. Morgan in his translation of the *Mirabilia* states that the legend of the Emperor's visit to the Sibyl first occurs in the *Chronographia* of Malalas, a writer of the sixth century.

[3]*Sub ara* is written over the line.

midst of the sun with her Son in her arms, depicted with angels, upon the wall above the high altar in the same church. Not far from this altar, are the following verses :

Stellat hinc in circulo Sibelle tunc oraculo, Te vidit rex in celo, O Mater dirige nos, et ad bonum erige pulso maligno telo, ora pro nobis scala tangens astra ne nos affligant damnator (*-um*) castrator(*es*) (*sic*).

" Subveniat quesumus domine plebi tue in periculis inclinate tua ut indiget miseracio copiosa ad quod te moveant Dei genetricis et sanctorum in presenti sarcophago sepultorum merita veneranda quorum memoriam deuocione qua possumus frequentamus per eundem[1]."

O Lord, we beseech Thee to assist with Thy abundant mercy Thy people in all dangers, moved thereto by the venerable merits of the Mother of God, and of the saints who are buried in this tomb, whose memory we celebrate to the best of our power, Through the same, etc.

Also, beneath the lower (*inferius*) altar of the same church—on the western side—is the following inscription :—

" Beneath this tabernacle resteth the body of the blessed Joan, sometime daughter of Franciscus de Felicibus ; " and, it is under the picture of the Virgin Mary.

---

[1]It is doubtful whether Brewyn copied the inscription correctly, at any rate the text is not easy to translate, the following is not much more than a free paraphrase :

> Shining within the mystic circle's rays
> The King beheld thee. All our ways
> Mother, direct, and thy blest help impart
> Turning aside the devil's deadly dart.
> Thou the tall ladder reaching to the sky,
> Pray that we be not lost eternally.

CONCERNING THE PICTURE OF ST. MARY* PAINTED BY ST. LUKE

Also, on a tablet, hanging near (the above) is the following inscription :—

" Cupientes scire aliquid et efficaciam huius sacre ymaginis Virginis Marie quam beatus Lucas evangelista depinxit, prout eam depingere cupiebat, picta tempore passionis, cum ante crucem laniatum filium deploraret, hanc scripturam legentes intellectualiter et retineant cum effectu, ante tamen omnia sciant fideles presentes literas inspecturi quod tempore beati Gregorii pape eximii doctoris in illa mortalitate magna que Romam adeo vehementi pestilencia laniavit[1], ut etiam corporali visu sagitte celitus venire, et singulos quosque percutere viderentur, que in mense xi veniens primum omnium percuscit papam Pellagium (ii. d. Feb. 8 590) et extinxit, igitur sine mora ordinata letania per leuitam Gregorium Septiformi illo, eodem die in tantum lues ipsa iudicio divino excrevit, et desevit, ut infra unius hore spacium, etiam dum voces plebs ad Dominum emitteret misericordiam invocando, octoginta homines at terram corruentes spiritum exalarent. In ista processione hac sacra ymagine deportata ecce aeris tum tribulencia cedebat ymagini, ac si ipsam ymaginem fugeret et eius presenciam nullatenus ferre posset, sicque post ymaginem mira serenitas et aeris pitas (? *puritas*) remanebat, tunc mire voces in aere cantencium et dicencium " Regina celi letare Alleluia " iuxta ymaginem sunt audite. Statim autem beatus Gregorius id quod sequitur adiunxit " Ora pro nobis Deum." Post hoc vidit beatus Gregorius supra castellum Crescensii[2] angelum qui revocabat in vagina

*Fo. 27b.

[1]An account of this plague is to be found in John the Deacon's Life of St. Gregory, Lib. l. 75 in Migne's Patr. Lat. vol. 75 and *De Gestis Langobardorum*, iii. c. 24.

[2]Fo. 28a. The tomb of Hadrian obtained the name of the Castle of Crescentius from the patrician who defended it against the Emperor Otho III, in 998. It was called the Castle of the Holy Angel before the eleventh century, and was connected with most of the outrages and factions which desolated Rome down to the end of the fourteenth century. Gregorovius, *op. cit.* iii, p. 520. Iv. p. 343.

gladium cruentatum, ex quo intellexit quod pestis illa cessasset, et sic factum est, et ideo illud castrum *Castrum Angeli* deinceps est vocatum, et ipse angelus cum gladio in vagina sculptus in lapide mire magnitudinis ab illo tempore vi antea invasit in cacumine dicti castri, inde tamen deiectus, sinistrante fortuna, per ictum machine obsidionis tempore per Romanos.

Est etiam ad memoriam revocandum ad plenam fidem omnium predictorum, quod in castri cacumine prelibati capella erat pulcherima ad honorem Angeli constructa, depictaque gloriose, ac etiam consecrata, et fortasse per dominum recolende memorie Nicholaum papam tercium (1277-1280) de domo Ursinorum, et erat ibi indulgencia singularis."

[Translation]

CONCERNING THE PICTURE OF ST. MARY PAINTED BY ST. LUKE

Also, on a tablet hanging near the above, is the following inscription :

The faithful who shall inspect these present letters, and are desirous of knowing something about the efficacy of the sacred picture of the Virgin Mary which blessed Luke, the evangelist, painted, even as he desired, namely, at the time of the Passion, as she was weeping before the cross over the mangled body of her Son ; and would understand, and remember, what they read, above all else should bear in mind, that in time of the illustrious doctor, blessed Gregory, the pope, during that great mortality which afflicted Rome with so much severity, the arrows of heaven seemed to be visible, even to the bodily eye, and to strike everyone. This plague which came in the xith month, smote and slew first of all pope Pelagius. Wherefore without delay a litany to be said by seven companies of people was ordained by the deacon (*levitum*) Gregory. Nevertheless, on the same day, to such an extent did the pestilence increase, and rage, that within the space of one hour, even as the people were lifting up their voices to the Lord, and imploring mercy, eighty men fell down and gave up the ghost. But when the sacred picture was carried in procession, lo, the aerial scourge yielded to the picture as though it fled from it, and could in no way endure its presence ; and so after the picture (had passed) the air remained wonderfully calm and pure. Then, strange to tell, voices from the sky were heard chanting near the picture and saying, "Rejoice, O Queen of heaven, Allelluia." To which blessed Gregory at once added, " Pray to God for us." After this blessed Gregory beheld above the castle of Crescencius[1] the angel sheathing his blood-stained sword, by which he understood that the plague had ceased, and so it proved to be. Wherefore henceforward the castle was called the Angel-Castle ; and a representation of the angel, with his sheathed sword was carved out of a great stone. From that time it occupied a position on the summit of the said castle ; but it was at length thrown down by an accidental blow from a missile which was discharged by the Romans during a siege.

Further it should be remembered that the very beautiful chapel at the top of the aforesaid castle, was built, gloriously painted, and, probably, consecrated also, in honour of the Angel, by Pope Nicholas III of revered memory, (1277-1280), of the house of the Ursini; here, too, there is a great indulgence.

Also, in the aforesaid Chapel there used to be a picture which showed completely the formation of this procession and litany[1].

And over the picture was written : " This is the sacred picture of the Heavenly Altar*."

[1]*Litania septiformis*, so called because those taking part in it were divided into seven parties or companies, viz. : Seculars, Monks, Laymen, Maidens, Married Women, Widows, and Paupers. See John the Deacon's *Life of St. Gregory* from which the above account is taken. Migne, Patr. Lat. vol. 75, Lib. I. p. 73. See also Gregory of Tours X.C.I., and Paul the Deacon in De Gestis Lang. III c. 24.

*Fo. 28b.

This account, and a representation of the procession, was depicted also in a certain chapel which is called St. Gregory's study, and is an appendage (*appendicium*) to the church of St. John Lateran.

Also, at the time of the great mortality in the year of the Lord mccclviii,[1] which began to afflict the city of Rome at the beginning of the month of June, and was at its full virulence during the month of August, this picture, with other relics, was, with due honour, devoutly carried through the city ; and when it reached the fount (*fontem*) of St. Peter the marble angel which is on the top of the castle showed reverence to this picture, by bowing to it several times, which miracle more than lx trustworthy men swore upon the holy gospels that they saw with their bodily eyes, while they were imploring the picture to have pity on them. There were, however, others who did not see the miracle, either because they were not worthy to do so or because their sight was not good enough, or, because they did not at the moment happen to look that way. Wherefore there was so much confusion that no one could give a clear account of the matter, and the best thing a man could do was to make what he could of the vision, and then bring out his goods and jewels and offer them before the picture, with the price of which the magnificent steps in front of the church were built[1].

Furthermore, to show how many miracles this picture has worked*, and how it has freed not a few people from many fatal perils, the lord Cardinal Peter de Columna[2] relates that when his ship was in danger,

---

[1]The text here is obscure, the latin is : " ob quam causam planctus omnium tantus erat quod nullus sufficeret ad narrandum, quapropter ille beatus erat qui expolire (*sic*) poterat et bona ante ipsam ymaginem producere, etc.

*Fo. 29a.   [2]Pietro Colonna, created Cardinal deacon of St. Eustace by Pope Nicholas IV, died at Avignon 1326.   The incident of his escape from shipwreck is mentioned by Cardella in his Memorie De' Cardinali etc. (Vol. II, p. 38), who adds that in gratitude for his escape, the Cardinal bestowed on the church of S. Maria Maggiore many valuable gifts.

owing to damage to the rudder, etc., he made an earnest prayer to this holy picture, and immediately the holy picture (exactly as depicted on the panel (*tabula*)) appeared in the sky close to the ship, from which apparition he felt confident that both he and his fellow travellers would speedily be delivered ; and forthwith they were wafted by favourable winds to their longed-for port. To this day a representation of this miracle remains, painted on the wall in front of (*ante*) the sacred picture itself.

All worshippers of Christ should pause devoutly here, because in the time of Gregory, by the goodness of Jesus (*bonitate Jesu*) this stone bears the impression of the Angel's feet[1].

THE STAIRWAY OF HEAVEN (SCALA COELI)

This is the second chapel[2]* that was founded in the whole world in honour of the Blessed Virgin Mary, and it is called the Stairway of Heaven because it was here that the blessed Bernard was deemed worthy to see the ladder which reached to heaven. Whosoever celebrates or causes a celebration to be made in this chapel for souls in purgatory, they (the said souls) for the merits of the same Blessed Virgin Mary shall speedily be set free, and whatsoever petition shall be devoutly made here shall surely be granted. For it was often said of old time, that whensoever masses for dear dead souls are celebrated here, they (the said souls) will at once be freed from the pains of purgatory.

[1]Dr. Holmes Dudden in his *Life of St. Gregory* states that the stone bearing the footprints is still to be seen in the Capitoline Museum. " It is," he says, " an altar dedicated to Isis by someone who had returned safely from a journey, which accordingly bears the conventional image of two foot-prints. The Altar at one time stood in the church of the *Ara Coeli* and the footprints —described by Peter de Winghe as those of a child of five years old—were long believed by Roman Christians to be those of the Angel seen by Gregory on the summit of Hadrian's Tomb." Life of St. Gregory, vol. I, p. 220.

[2]S. Maria Della Scala.

*Fo. 29b.

It should be remembered that in the church of St. Athanasius, the martyr, there are indulgences every day of seven thousand years[1].

Also, by pope Urban the third, one thousand and five hundred years of enjoined penances are mercifully relaxed. Pope Silvester also granted a like number, and pope Gregory a like number, also Nicholas (sic) granted one year.

Also, Pope Gregory mercifully granted to all and singular, who shall visit the said church of St. Anastasius, the martyr, as pilgrims, at any time of the year, or the Salvian Waters (*Aquas Salvias*) near the church of St. Anastasius, either out of reverence for St. Paul, or for prayer or pilgrimage, (if he be not in mortal sin), the blotting out of forgotten and venial sins, as well as the offences of fathers and mothers, without imposition of hands[2]. Moreover, in the same church of St. Anastasius, according to the ancient canons, there is an indulgence of xl thousand years.

Also, at *Aquae Salviae** on the anniversary of the consecration of the same church, there is remission of all sins, viz. : on the xxxth of January.

THE CHAPEL SCALA CELI[3].

It was found by our predecessors of old time in certain writings that the second chapel which was founded in honour of Holy Mary, is the church of St. Mary of the Heavenly Stairway, in which beneath the altar, repose ten thousand bodies of saints and martyrs slain in the time of the emperor Tiberius, who, in defence of the faith, fought against the pagans on the

[1]The Church St. Athanasius at Trefontane was given by Innocent II in 1140 to St. Bernard, who founded there a Cistercian Monastery.

[2]The present practice is for the priest in absolution to stretch out his hand in the direction of the penitent, in medieval times, he placed his hands upon the head of the penitent.

*Fo. 30a.

[3]Scala Coeli at Trefontane.

hill called the Holy Mount, which is between the monastery of St. Paul and (the church of) St. Anastasius.

Also, in order to increase the respect due to this most holy church, it has been proved many times by those who have made the trial, that whosoever shall devoutly drink of the three fountains where blessed Paul, the apostle, was beheaded, shall be freed from whatsoever infirmity may afflict him. Also, it is said, that here there are indulgences of a thousand years.

In the northern chapel of the same church of St. Anastasius, are the four heads of the captains of the aforesaid three thousand martyrs, namely: Saints Agacius, Hemolaus, Alexander and Mark.

Also, in the same chapel, is the marble column (*columna*) upon which the head of St. Paul, the apostle, was cut off; it stands in a recess within (*infra*) the wall, and a chain hangs in front (*ante*) of this pillar.

The Friars of this place are wont to ask and receive one bezant (*beacum*) for celebrating the mass, etc.

THE CHURCH OF THE HOLY CROSS*

This venerable and most noble church of the Holy Cross[1], Constantina, daughter of the Emperor, built to the honour of the most adorable Holy Cross, and, at the request of the blessed Helen, mother of the said Emperor Constantine.

Silvester, pope of the city of Rome (*sic*), consecrated it in the year and on the day above named. (*The date is not given*).

The relics in this urn of basalt which forms the great and principal altar[2] of this church, are the bodies of St. Anastasius and Cesarius, and the indulgence

*Fo. 30b.
[1] S. Croce in Gerusalemme.
[2] Reliquie in hac concha *pagonis* (for *paragonis*) quod (*sic*) est magnum altare et principale huius ecclesie.

from this source, is xl years, and as many quarantines —on each day of the year.

Also, on the feast of the consecration of the same church an indulgence of xxii years begins, and as many quarantines.

On each day of the year there are seven years and seven quarantines.

On every Sunday, and fourth weekday throughout the year, blessed Silvester, the aforesaid pope, at the request of the blessed Helen, doubled all indulgences to those who shall visit the church; or, granted indulgences so great that they do actually double all the aforesaid indulgences. The sum of all the indulgences is : On all Sundays and fourth days of the week throughout the year cxxxvi years, and as many quarantines, without taking count of the indulgence granted on the feast of the Invention and Exaltation of the Cross, and all these (*indulgences*) stand good throughout the octaves, except with regard to the remission of a third part of all sins.

Also, it is recorded that Pope Silvester, Pope Gregory, Pope Alexander, Pope Nicholas, Pope Pellagius and Pope Honorius* gave to all, who at any time of the year, shall come for devotion and pilgrimage to the holy places in Rome, amongst which is this one, an indulgence of a thousand years, and to those who shall die on the journey the remission of all their sins[1].

On the feast of St. Caesarius—which is on the feast of All Saints, and on that of St. Anastasius—which is on the xxii day of January, there is remission of a fourth part of all sins.

THE LORD'S TITLE (*titulus dominicus*).

The title of the Lord's cross on which is written : " Hic est IHS Nazarenus rex iudeorum " has been

*Fo. 31a.

hidden away in the sham window which is painted
over the arch in the middle of the church[1] on its outer
face[2] ; and across it (*extraverso*) is an arm of the cross
of the robber, who, when he was crucified with
Christ, said, " Remember me, etc."

IN THE SACRISTS' CHAPEL[3]

The wood of the most holy Cross, together with
one of the nails with which Christ was crucified on the
cross, and many other relics of the saints, are laid up
very reverently in the Sacrists' chapel, which is near
the pulpit (*tribunam*) of the above-named Church of
the Holy Cross ; in which the monks of the Carthusian
Order, both by day and night, perform divine service,
and celebrate their masses. And it[4] (the holy relic) is
shown five times in the year, that is to say, on Good
Friday, on the feasts of the Invention and Exaltation,
on the day of the Station, and of the dedication of the
same church of the Holy Cross, and on the (*Day of*)
the consecration of the Jerusalem chapel—on the above
named days and seasons*.

CONCERNING THE JERUSALEM CHAPEL[5]

This most sacred and venerable chapel, which is
called the Jerusalem Chapel, the blessed Helen, the

[1]S. Croce.

[2]The latin here is : Est reconditus in illa fenestra incancelata que supra
archum in medio ecclesie in exteriore facie depicta. The title written in three
languages was found walled up in one of the Arches of the Apse during
some restorations undertaken by Cardinal Mendoza in 1492. *Christian and
Ecclesiastical Rome*, Tuker and Malleson.

[3]S. Croce.

[4]The Carthusians were established at S. Croce by Urban V. c. 1370, and
remained there until the time of Pius IV (1559-1566) who removed the
Carthusians and put in their place the Cistercians of S. Sabba.

*Fo. 31b.

[5]The chapel of St. Helena in the crypt of the Church. The vault of this
chapel is adorned with mosaics said to date from the Emperor Valentinian
III (425) but much restored.

mother of the Emperor Constantine, built in what aforetime was her bed-chamber (*cubiculum*). And the blessed Silvester, the pope, adorned and sanctified this chapel on the xxth day of the month of March, on the eve of St. Benedict's day. And the notable relics, which are recorded below, were laid up in the altar of the aforesaid chapel by the hands of blessed Silvester, at the request of the aforesaid Helen, which relics, the blessed Helen herself brought from Jerusalem, at the request of the aforesaid Pope.

First, the cord with which Christ was bound on the Cross.

Two sapphires, one of which is full of the precious blood of Christ, and the other of the milk of the glorious Virgin Mary, the Mother of Christ.

Also a large piece of Christ's garment ; a large piece of the veil of the mother of Mary, the Mother of Christ; a large piece of Christ's garment (*probably repeated by mistake*) ; some of the hair of the Blessed Virgin Mary ; the sponge together with the salt and vinegar that were offered to Christ.

Also, xi thorns of the Lord's crown ; a large piece of the garment of St. John the Baptist ; the fore-arms of the blessed Apostles Peter and Paul ; a lump (*massa*), like a loaf, formed of coal ashes and the fat of the blessed Laurence, the martyr ; a lamp filled with sweet oil (*balsamo*), in which floats the head of blessed Vincent, the martyr.

In the said chapel there is daily an indulgence of xxvii years and xxvii quarantines, which begins on the fourth day of the week before Passion Sunday, and lasts throughout the whole year.

Also, Pope Stephen, who died here, gave an indulgence of all sins to all who come hither truly penitent and confessed.

Also, on the day of the consecration of the said

chapel, there is the true eternal promise, and remission of all sins.

Further, on every sixth day of the week, that is to say, on all Fridays throughout the whole year—if (the visit) be continued throughout in true penitence—there is an indulgence from both penance (*pena*) and guilt (*culpa*), especially on Good Friday, as was set forth, and is still set forth on the wall in letters formed of mosaic work, depicted or displayed over the altar of the said Jerusalem chapel.

Also, into the said Jerusalem chapel, women ought not to enter throughout the whole year, except on the day of the consecration of the same chapel, which, as is stated above, was consecrated on the xxth day of the month of March, on the eve of St. Benedict the Abbot.

Also, on that altar no one may celebrate save the Pope only. Its beauty is in no way remarkable.

Also, on a tablet (*tabula*) over the altar—on the right hand side as you enter the church of the Holy Cross—is the following inscription :

" In this altar are the relics of many saints, to wit : The finger of blessed Adrian ; two teeth of blessed Blaise ; some of the bones of the blessed Mary Magdalene and other saints. This altar was consecrated in honour of blessed Michael, the archangel, and of the above-mentioned saints ; and there are indulgences of vii years and vii quarantines on the xiii day of March, and they last throughout the whole year*.

THE RELICS AND INDULGENCES OF THE ALTAR[1]

Also, on a tablet on the left hand side, I found the following inscription : " This altar contains the relics of many saints, namely, of blessed Gregory, the Pope, blessed Hilary, blessed John the Baptist, and of

*Fo. 32b.
[1]S. Croce.

several other saints." This altar was consecrated in honour of the saints whose relics are laid up therein. The indulgences are vii years and vii quarantines. It should be noted also, that in this church is a picture of the Saviour, which is called the picture of divine compassion (*pietatis*).

Also, this church is remarkable for its beautiful pavement formed of stones of divers colours artistically arranged. Outside the gate of this church lies a great stone upon which, as is said, Pope Stephen was beheaded (A.D. 257).

Also, near the church of the Holy Cross, as pilgrims make their way to the church of the St. John Lateran, there is a place resembling a small chapel, on the wall of which is painted a picture of St. Mary the Virgin, which, as the inscription states, and according to common report, addressed the blessed Gregory as he was passing by the spot in a procession, wherefore great honour is shown to this picture.

Also, in the church of the Holy Cross there are three pieces, parts, or blocks (*massae*) of the most precious wood of the Lord's cross ; and each one has a colour peculiar to itself. The first is of a whitish tint (*aliqualiter alba*) all over, the second is almost black (*quasi nigra*), and the third whiter than the one first mentioned ; and they are shown in a silver casket (*jocali de argento*) fashioned like an arch.

Also, there is a nail with which the Lord was crucified, which is almost entire.

Also, the aforesaid picture of divine compassion has the head leaning upon (*super*) the right shoulder, and the right hand clasped over the left.

Also, at the church of SS. Sebastian and Fabian, in a chapel, there is another picture very much like this one ; there are also many such pictures at Rome, though none quite so large as this one.

F

THE CHURCH OF SS. SEBASTIAN AND FABIAN[1]

Be it known to all and singular of Christ's faithful servants who either now or in the future, shall look upon this page and what is written therein, that in this holy and most worshipful church of the holy martyrs Sebastian and Fabian, there are on every day indulgences, almost innumerable.

The first thing to be noticed is the place where the body of S. Sebastian lieth, namely, in the lower altar, where St. Gregory, the pope, as he was celebrating saw the angel of God, who, as he (*Gregory*) was performing the solemn office of the mass, said to him, " This is the most holy place in which is the true promise and the remission of all sins, the splendour of perpetual light and joy without end, all which Christ's martyr Sebastian won." Therefore, whosoever as a pilgrim shall at any time of the year visit this church for prayer or pilgrimage, shall have without fail the said indulgence, namely, the one which was declared by the angel and confirmed by St. Gregory*.

Also, in the higher (*superiori*) altar lieth the body of St. Fabian, pope and martyr.

Also, Pope Pelagius granted on every day xlviii years of indulgences and as many quarantines, to all who shall come here.

Also, an indulgence of full remission of all sins is given, as has already been stated, to all who shall visit the church either for prayer or pilgrimage, on all Sundays throughout the month of May.

Also, from the Lord's Ascension to the Kalends of August, on every day there are in the aforesaid church M/xiiii(14000) years of salutary (*salutaribus*) indulgences.

Also, Pope Gregory, Pope Silvester, Pope Alexander, Pope Nicholas, Pope Pelagius, Pope Honorius, and

[1]On the Via Appia, the church is attributed to Constantine.
*Fo. 33b.

Pope John granted each one separately, seven thousand years of indulgences to all pilgrims who shall come to this church for the above mentioned purposes.

Also, in the cemetery of St. Kalixtus, which is underground, the bodies of xlvi of the chief pontiffs were buried, each one of whom bequeathed an ample blessing with indulgences. Now, in the aforesaid cemetery, where many bodies of saints, martyrs, confessors and virgins are buried, there is plenary remission from penance (*pena*) and guilt (*culpa*), on every day, as is stated in the register (*cronico*)*

Further, one reads in the legend of St. Sebastian that any pilgrim who shall die when visiting this church, shall retain all the aforesaid remissions for the merits of St. Sebastian, the martyr. It should be noted, however, that the body of St. Stephen, pope and martyr, lieth near the altar, but at the back of it (*retro*)— where the iron grate is—and here there are seven years of indulgences and as many quarantines.

Also, in the Catacomb there is a well behind the church, in which the bodies of SS. Peter and Paul remained hidden away for CC and LII (252) years ; out of reverence for whom, on every day, indulgences were given by Pope Silvester, which are as great as those given in the church of St. Peter the Apostle. Now all the more recent indulgences of the said church are doubled in Lent and on double and triple feasts, and above all on the feasts of the saints who are commemorated here.

THE RELICS OF THIS CHURCH[1]

The body of St. Sebastian, the martyr, lies in the lower altar where St. Gregory, the pope, as he was celebrating mass, saw the angel of God, who said to him as he was performing the holy service of mass :

*Fo. 34a.
[1]SS. Sebastian and Fabian.

" This is the most holy place in which is the true promise, the remission of all sins, the splendour of perpetual light, and joy without end, all which Sebastian, Christ's martyr, won,"—as is stated in the bull of Clement the sixth (1342-1352) concerning the year of Jubilee. Further, it is believed that whosoever shall celebrate upon the above named altar, or shall cause another so to do shall free (*a soul*) from the pains of purgatory.

Also, near the said altar—where the iron cross is— resteth the body of Lucina, the glorious virgin[1] a very noble Roman Lady, who buried the body of St. Sebastian, the martyr, in the said place, and built this church in honour of the same Sebastian.

Also, in an altar which is near by,—in the upper part (of the church) (*in parte superiori*) lieth the body of St. Fabian, pope and martyr ; the head of St. Stephen, pope and martyr ; the head of St. Kalixtus, pope and martyr ; the head of St. Acorist, martyr ; the head of St. Valentina, virgin and martyr ; the head of St. Nereus, martyr ; the head of St. Lucy, virgin ; one thorn of Christ's crown ; one finger of St. Peter, the apostle ; one rib of St. Peter the apostle ; one tooth of St. Peter, the apostle ; one finger of St. Paul the apostle ; an arm of St. Sebastian the martyr ; one tooth of St. Paul the apostle ; one rib of St. Paul the apostle ; also, two of the darts or arrows of the martyr Sebastian; one piece of the arm of St. Andrew, the apostle ; one small fragment (*frustrum*) of St. Christopher, the martyr ; also the bodies of the seven sleepers which were found in the time of Pope Kalixtus* the third (1447-1458) ; also the stone on which Christ left the impression of His feet, when He met Peter, the apostle, at the place which is called " *Domine quo vadis.*"[2]

And, at the spot where Christ met Peter, there is a cross, and at the place where Christ ascended into

---

[1]Generally described as a matron.

*Fo. 35a.

heaven, there is a chapel, having an altar in the midst of it.

And, at the gates through which this road enters the city of Rome, there are, I believe, on the walls xviii or more snow-balls (*pilae nivis*) which those who took St. Peter threw at him, and they still may be seen there looking exactly like snow-balls.

IN THE CHURCH OF ST. LAURENCE OUTSIDE THE WALLS[1]

Hic sita (sunt) uno sanctissima corpora busto
Que duo martyrii rutilas meruere coronas
Extat primus honor Stephanas, Laurencius alter
Posterus ad poenas[2] sed acutum primus ob ignem
Pervigil et dextera recubat Iustinius in urna
Marmore quadrato qui texit cespite passos.
Tum bene cardinei sepelibant corpora patres,
Et cava cripta docet quot millia condidit iste.
Tu modo flecte genu Laurencius ob pia vota
Liberat hic animas purgandas tristibus umbris.[3]

[Translation]

Entombed together here two martyrs rest
Two golden crowns their sanctity attest.
Stephen and Laurence—but the first in name
Yields place to him who faced the searing flame.
Justin, who laid the sufferers neath the sward,
On yonder marble hearse keeps watch and ward :
This nobler tomb the fathers built, and deep
In vaulted crypt uncounted numbers sleep.
Here bow the knee, for Laurence not in vain
Sues for unshriven souls and breaks their chain.

[1]The Liber pontificalis and the biographies of S. Silvester attribute this church to Constantine, it was restored by Pope Pelagius II, on the occasion of the translation of the body of St. Stephen from Constantinople to Rome.

[2]Poems in the text.

[3]The vith lesson for the feast of St. Laurence (Aug. 10) in the Sarum Breviary concludes thus : " Justinius presbyter cum Ipolito . . . corpus beati Laurentis tulerunt et in presidium matronae viduae Ciriaci via Tiburtina asportaverunt et facto vespere, in cripta quae erat in verano quarto idus Augusti sepelierunt." Pope Nicholas V (1447-1455) sent five cardinals to investigate the alleged discovery by the Friars Minor in Rome, of the body of St. Laurence within the precincts of their house, who, after doing so, pronounced the body to be the veritable body of St. Laurence and reburied it. Martene *Vet. Script.* vol. IV, Col. 1216.

The Sum of the indulgences granted here by blessed Silvester, the pope, in the time of the Emperor Constantine, and by blessed Pelagius, the Pope (578-590) who consecrated this church, and by other chief pontiffs, are daily, a thousand years, and as many quarantines, and the remissions of a third part of all sins.

In Lent, and on the feasts of SS. Stephen and Laurence, on Station days, and on the sixth day of the week before Palm Sunday, the indulgences are doubled.

On the feasts of SS. Stephen and Laurence, there is plenary remission of all sins. Thanks be to God. In this place also certain fair (pulchra) relics are shown at divers seasons, namely :

The bowl in which Tiburcius was baptized by St. Laurence ; the stone that is said to be one of those with which St. Stephen was stoned, and it is a very fine stone and one of remarkable appearance.

There are also many other things which I am unable to name.

Also, in Rome is St. Laurence's house, or the place where he gave to the poor the treasure of the church (*dedit pauperibus thesauro ecclesie (sic)*) ; and, near the entrance to the place there is a little spring beneath the surface of the ground (*sub introitum terrae*), full of water. Also, in the aforesaid house is the gridiron upon which St. Laurence was roasted, it is beautifully ornamented with gilded silver, etc.

THE CHURCH OF SS. COSMAS AND DAMIAN[1]

Whosoever shall visit this venerable church, namely, the church of SS. Cosmas and Damian, shall have, on every day, the thousand years of indulgences that were granted by blessed Gregory the first. The same St.

[1]The Church of SS. Cosmas and Damian, was built on the Via Sacra by Felix IV, (A.D. 526-529) on the site of the temple of Romulus. It was the first Church to be built in the heart of pagan Rome (*Gregorovius, op. cit.* Vol. I, p. 345).

Gregory consecrated the high altar of this church, and, with his own hands, laid up beneath that altar the bodies of the saints Cosmas and Damian, Antimus, Leoncius and Euphrasius, and an arm of St. Matthew, the apostle.

Also, whosoever, shall visit the chapel of St. Mary the virgin in the said church, which is behind the high altar, shall have a hundred and sixty days of indulgence for every day, and on the feasts of St. Mary and during the octaves of the same these indulgences are doubled.

Also, in the sacristy of this church a little coffer is preserved, in which are many venerable relics. In the first place, a phial of glass containing the milk of the Virgin Mary.

Some of the hair of St. Mary Magdalene ; some of the hair of Abra ; some of the relics of St. Sebastian, the martyr ; some of the cloak (*pallium*) of St. Giles, the abbot ; some of the crown of St. Thomas ; some of the relics of St. Martina, the Virgin ; some of the relics of SS. Nereus and Achilles ; some of the relics of SS. Cosmas and Damian ; some of the wood of the true cross ; some of the veil of the Blessed Virgin Mary ; some of the relics of St. Denys, the martyr ; one of the clubs with which St. Theodore was slain ; some of the relics of St. Boniface, the martyr ; and of St. Philip, the apostle.

Also, some of the relics of St. Alexander the martyr ; of Pope Leo, of St. Rufus, the martyr ; of St. Just, the virgin ; also, a piece of one of the thorns of the crown of our Lord Jesus Christ*.

Some of what was burnt by the fire which came down from the veritable holy stone (*a proprio sancto lapide*) of the tomb of our Lord Jesus Christ ; and many other relics which are unlabelled (*sine scriptura*). In this most venerable basilica which is called the church of SS. Cosmas and Damian, on the floor of the

*Fo. 36b.

choir, within a circle are these verses, inscribed in letters formed of mosaic work :

Aula Dei claris radiat speciosa[1] metallis,
In qua plus[2] fidei lux preciosa micat.
Martiribus Medicis populo spes certa salutis
Venit, et ex[3] sacro crevit honore locus.
Obtulit hoc domino Felix antistite dignum
Munus ut aetheria[4] vivat in arce poli.

[Translation]

Bright gleam the jewels in this holy shrine ;
More precious gleam the rays of Faith divine.
Here martyr, healer, citizen, have shed
Eternal hope and glory where we tread.
This princely gift by holy Felix given
Has found its guerdon in the halls of heaven.

In the church of St. Clement[5] are the following relics :

Within the altar of the church of St. Clement is the body of St. Clement, pope and martyr, which was brought across the sea from the city of Cersosa[6], and it was translated to this city by the most christian and indulgent Emperor Justinian ; here also are the relics of many other saints.

An arm of St. Clement is in the church of SS. Marcellin and Peter.

In this church also are many indulgences, and a third part of all sins is here graciously remitted by pope Alexander.

[1]The text is very corrupt here.   sponsa. [2]pius. [3]hoc. [4]ethea. The inscription is given by Gregorovius and also by Dom Leclercq. Gregorovius states that the inscription now forms a frame to the picture of the Saviour on the tribune.

[5]The church of St. Clement is mentioned by St. Jerome in his *De Viris illustribus*, about 385. The basilican church was rebuilt in the XII century. Excavations undertaken in 1857 have revealed the existence of the earlier church beneath the present structure. Taker and Malleson *op. cit.*

[6]Chersonese, i.e. the Crimea, to which region Pope Clement was banished.

THE CHURCH OF ST. BARTHOLOMEW[1]

In the church of St. Bartholomew*, the apostle, which is situated upon, or within (*supra vel infra*) the Tiber, are the following relics :

First, the body of St. Bartholomew, the apostle of Jesus Christ.

The body of blessed Paulinus, the confessor of Christ [d. 431] of the church of Nola, of whom blessed Gregory makes mention in his Dialogues[2]. The bodies of Marcellus and Superancius, the martyrs.

The chin of St. James, the greater, the apostle.

The arms of the holy apostles, Symon and Jude.

One of the thorns of the crown of our Lord Jesus Christ.

Three of the arrows which were aimed at, and were extracted from the body of St. Sebastian, the glorious martyr.

An arm of St. Adelbert, bishop and martyr.

An arm of St. James, the less, apostle.

Some of the wood of the true cross of our Lord Jesus Christ.

Certain relics of SS. Menna and Felicitas, and of other saints, martyrs and confessors.

THE CHURCH OF ST. CECILIA[3]

In the Church of St. Cecilia[4] on the other side of the Tiber, which was formerly the saint's house are the following relics :

[1]The Church of S. Bartolomeo All Isola which was originally dedicated to SS. Adelbert and Paulinus was built over the ruins of the temples of Aesculapius and Jupiter upon the island in the Tiber in the tenth century. It was much damaged by floods in 1557, and was rebuilt by Gregory XIII (1572-1585).

*Fo. 37a.

[2]Liber iv, de miraculis patrum Italicorum.

[3]St. Cecilia in Transtevere. [4]According to the Acts of St. Cecilia, the church occupied the site of the house of Valerian, the husband of the saint and is said to date from the pontificate of Urban I (223-230). The house was almost entirely destroyed when the church was reconstructed early in the ninth century by Pope Paschal I. The church was restored in 1283 and again in 1599.

Within the high altar is the body of St. Cecilia, virgin and martyr; the bodies of SS. Tiburcius and Valerian; Urban the first; Lucius the first, and Maximus. Also, the bodies of nine hundred and forty martyrs which were taken out of the cemetery of Kalixtus, and laid up here by Pope Paschal, who rebuilt this church after it had been destroyed by the Lombards[1] (*magotis*), and he granted to all confessed and contrite persons who shall visit the church, and give alms, an indulgence of a hundred years, as many quarantines, and the remission of a third part of all sins. This is recorded in the official registry (*registerio judic*) at St. Peter's in the fair city of Rome.*

And I, William Brewyn, chaplain, give thanks to God.

THE CHURCH OF ST. MARY ON THE OTHER SIDE OF THE TIBER[2]

In the church of St. Mary[3] on the other side of the Tiber, are these relics :

First, some of the Lord's table; some of the hair of the Virgin Mary; the cloak of Bishop Theodore, the martyr[4]; some of the dress of the Virgin Mary, to wit, some of the leather of her shoe, and some of her dalamatic.

Also (something) of the martyrs, Ciriac, Largus, Smaragdus, Policonius, Adorius, Romana, the virgin, Nereus, the martyr, Lucia and Geminianus, Agapitus, Cromacius, Passara, Secundus, and Argenius, Hillarius, Papiens, Pudenciana, the virgin; Mary, Martha, Audifax, Abacuch, Pontus, Marcellus, and Peter.

[1] A.D. 755.

* Fo. 37b.

[2] Built by Pope Julius I (337-352), it is called in the *Liber Pontificalis* " Basilica Julia juxta Callistum." The Church was almost entirely rebuilt by Innocent II in 1130, and has suffered much from subsequent restorations.

[3] S. Maria in Transtevere.

[4] *Virginis* has been written by mistake for *martiris*.

Austerius, martyr, Felix, SS. Attica and Artemia, virgins ; Pantanus, abbot, Symphrosa with her seven sons, Benedict and Sebastian, Peregrina, virgin and martyr ; Martina, virgin ; Donatus, martyr, Ambrose[1].

Also, the relics of very many other martyrs whose names are not set forth.

Jesus have mercy upon me.

PAPAL EXCOMMUNICATION

Here follow certain excommunications which Pope Paul (1469-1471) with his cardinals, archbishops and bishops, who are said to have numbered lxiii, in the hearing of William Brewyn, chaplain, who was present at the time, pronounced, to wit, in the city of Rome, at the door of the church of St. Peter the apostle, upon all transgressors such as are specified below, and not only upon those, but in truth on very many others also.

The denunciation was pronounced by two cardinals, who stood near the pope, one on his right hand, and the other on his left, and that denunciation lasted for a full hour by the clock of St. Peter. And many of them (*the prelates*) I am not certain about all, held in their hands great lighted wax candles, which they cast down between (*inter*) the feet of the bystanders in token of their contempt and reprobation of those who were thus excommunicated, and this took place in Rome in the year of the Lord MCCCCLXIX according to the English way of reckoning, to wit, on Thursday in Holy Week.

And I, the aforesaid William, copied the excommunication which here followeth, from the bull of the lord Pope Paul as it was hanging over the door of the church of St. Peter the apostle, on Easter Eve[2] :

[1]The words *Arothe Medos* follow possibly for *Archiepi Mediolani*.
[2]Paul II (1464-1471) in 1470 reduced the interval between the recurrence of the papal Jubilee to twenty-five years : the period had been previously reduced by Pope Urban VI to thirty-three years. Cocqueline's *Bullarum Collectio* Tom iii, p. 128.

Excommunicamus et anathematizamus omnes muti-
lantes vulnerantes seu interficientes vel capientes vel
detinentes seu depredantes Romipetas et peregrinos
ad urbem causa peregrinacionis et devotionis acce-
dentes et ea morantes et recedentes ab ipsa, et hiis
dantes auxilium vel favorem, eorumque bona confis-
camus, etc.

Licet plures Romani Pontifices nostri predecessores
diversis ecclesiis et piis locis indulgencias plenarias
concesserint et felicis recordacionis Pius, papa secundus
immediatus eciam predecessor noster legitimus, ex
causis et presertim ut melius reipublice Christiane
consuleretur, et contra Turchos ferventius intenderent
eas suspenderit, nos que eciam eisdem ex causis
s u s p e n c i o n e m ipsam conprobaverimus et gratam
habuerimus prout approbamus et gratam havemus
illam que ad beneplacitum A p o s t o l i c e s e d i s
perdurare decrevimus tum sicut pluriorum relacione
fidedignorum querelanter accepimus, nonnulli iniqui-
tatis filii ordinacionum et mandatorum Apostolicorum
contemptores, atque ipsius reipublice Christiane non
minus quam ipse Turchus iniuncti, in suarum animarum
et aliarum fidelium grave periculum indulgencias,
huiusmodi tanquam non suspensas predicare et
publicare presumunt.

Nos igitur ad huiusmodi rebellionem refrenenendam
excommunicamus, et anathematizamus omnes et
singulos qui sic suspensas indulgencias deincips
quovismodo publicantes, vel predicantes, aut illis
utentes locorum ordinariis* sub similibus sentenciis
censuris et penis, quas contrafaciendo ipso facto
incurrant harum serie iniungentes ne in eorum civi-
tatibus et diocesis similes indulgencias publicari vel
predicari faciant vel permittant, a presentibus autem
censuris et penis, quoque casus prescriptos secuntur,
sexum omnino nullum condicionem hominum
nullam exumimus (? *exuimus*) non patriarchas, non

*Fo. 38b.

archiepiscopos, non episcopos, non cuiuscumque generis prelatos non reges non reginas, non duces, non machiones[1], non comites, non ullius alterius dignitatis, vel presidentes, velut quemque privatum ita eos abnoxios esse et reos presencium censuarum decernimus, nolentes privilegium ullum, ullam indulgenciam, ullas apostolicas, vim quamcumque verborum habentes processibus hiis nostris obstare.

Rogamus omnipotentem et misericordem Deum et suppliciter deprecamur, ut animas que vinculis harum censurarum ligate non sunt, ne ligentur, conservet que vero ligate sunt ad salutem et meritum absolucionis convertat. Nos tum ipsam absolucionem nobis t-amen et successoribus nostris romanis pontificibus reservamus, articulo mortis dumtaxat excepto, vi quo eciam satisfaccionem et caucionem canonicam ab eis esse volumus esse (*sic*) exigendas. Simili excommunicatione innodantes sacerdotes illos tam seculares quam cuiusvis ordinis Regulares qui sit excommunicatos et anathematizatos eciam in ipso mortis articulo constitutos, aliter quam prefertur, absolverint eisque predicatorum, lectorum, administratorum sacrorum, auditorum confessionum, interdicimus per presentes etc. Nulli igitur omnino liceat hanc paginam nostrorum excommunicacionum, anathematizacionis, confiscacionis, donacionis, sublacionis revocacionis innodacionis, interdicti et prediccionis, infringere, vel ei ausu temerario contraire. Si autem, etc. infert malediccionem Dei omnipotentis etc. secundum communem modum literarum papalium.

Further, the Pope after making the above denunciation, granted to all who were there present, plenary remission of all sins in the form adopted by the church, giving them the blessing of the Father, the Son and the Holy Ghost, and his own, and then with

---

[1] *Sic* for *marchiones.*

his attendants, he departed in peace. In Christ Jesus
our Lord, Amen.

Deo Ihu gracias. (rubricated).

*   *   *

THE ROUTE (via) FROM CALAIS TO ROME*

From Calais to Gravenyng (Gravelines)   iii miles
To Merdyk   ii miles
To Dunkyrk   i long (mile), it is a good town.
To Newport (Nieuport)   v miles. A good town and
    walled.
To Ostende   ii miles. Money, plakks and stufyrs.
To Dwdyngborgh (Doudenborg)   ii miles.
To Bruggys (Bruges)   iii miles ; a very good town and
    well . . . *(cut off by binder).*
To Herse   iii miles
To Gaunte (Gand)   iiii miles ; it is a good walled-
    town.
To Dyndyrmowthe[1] (Dendermonde)   v miles.
To Makelyn (Mechlin)   v miles ; it is a good town
    and walled.
To Arstok (Aerschot)   iiii miles.
To Dys (Diest)   iii miles.
To Halyn or Hakyn (Heelen)   half a mile.
To Herk (Herck)   i mile.
To Halsyll (Hasselt)   ii miles.
To Bylsyn (Bilsen)   ii miles.
To Mastreyth (Maestricht)   ii miles, and, it is a good
    walled town.
To Gulpyn (Gulpen)   ii miles, under the little hill (*sub
    monticulam*), a dangerous road on account of . . .
    (cut off by binder)[2].

*Fo. 40a.
[1]Brabancia in margin.
[2]Suabia in margin.

To Akon (Aachen) ii miles ; it is a good town or
city and there is a great pilgrimage to St. Mary's
because her shift is there in the hall . . . (*cut off
by binder*).

To Gulyk or Gulk iiii miles ; Colysch money . . . or
whyt pens for one . . . penny . . . (*cut off by binder*).

To Berkham (Bergheim) iii miles.

To the city of Cologne iii miles. Here lie the three
holy Kings and the xi thousand virgins.

To Bune (Bonn) iiii miles. Here are " fals shrewys
summe " unless they have become better (*nisi
meliorantur*)*.

To Remark (Remagen) iiii miles.

To Andyrnak (Andernach) iii miles. A good town
per . . . (?).

To Coualens (Coblens) iii miles.

To Bokard, or Bobard (Boppart) iii miles.

To Wesyl iii miles.

To Barag i mile.

To Benge (Bingen) ii miles.

To Mens or Maguncia (Mainz) v miles, good.

To Upnaham or Uppungham (Oppenheim) iii miles.

To Wurmys (Worms) iiii miles.

To Hotte iii miles.

To Speer (Speyer) iii miles, Blafforth or Remysh
(*money*) money beyond the Rhine.

To Brushell (Brushshal) beyond the Rhine or Bemysh
iii miles.

To Breton (Bretton) ii miles.

To Mulborum (Maad-bronn) i mile.

To Faynger (Vachingen) ii miles.

To Swapertyng i mile.

To Constant (Constadt) ii miles.

To Esselyng (Esslingen) ii miles.

To Gyppyng (Goppingen) iii miles.

To Gyssling (Gelssingen) ii miles.

*Fo. 4ob.

To Ulmys (Ulm)   A beautiful city, iii miles, show the
   tonsured head to escape the tax (*monstra coronam
   capitis pro tributo*).
To Memmyng (Memmingen)   vi miles ; it is a fine
   city. The Road is said to be fairly good, but
   further on the mountains begin*.
To Kempton   iiii miles. A good walled town.
To Nessylwang   ii miles.
To Fyls (Vyls)   ii miles.
To Attylwang   ii miles.
To Lermos (Lermoos)   ii miles.
To Nazaret (Nassereut)   ii miles.
To Honyst (? Imst)   ii miles.
To Sammys   ii miles.
To Landyk   half a mile.
To Brotys   ii miles.
To Fovus   ii miles.
To Nawdyrs   ii miles.
To Mals   iii miles.
To Slawnders   ii miles.
To Slactys   i mile.
To Merane   iiii miles. Take note of the market.
To Sepawle   iii miles.
To Caldyre (Kaltern)   i mile.
To Tremyn (Tramen)   i mile.
To Salarium (Salurn)   i mile.
To Mount St. Nicholas   i mile ; it is strewed with
   inns (*est stratum hospiciis*).
To Trent   ii miles ; it is a good town and walled.
To Gallyan (Calliano)   viii miles.
To Reuereyt (Roveredo)   iiii miles (*miliaria lumbard,*'
   in margin).
To Ala   x miles†.
To Dulce (Dolce)   iii miles.
To Cluke or Luce   xii miles.
To Porone   (*Mileage not given*).

*Fo. 41a.
†Fo. 41b.

To Verona, a fine city xii miles, multi Lumbard (written over the line) Here one is given " bylles " or staves (*baculos*).

To Scala   xii miles.

To Nugarer (Nogara)   viii miles.

To Hostia (Ostiglia)   x miles ; one ought to be ferried across the water[1] for one crucifer.

To Pulp   x miles, I think it is.

To Bonpert   iii miles ; one should give a crucifer for the ship or boat[2].

To Bologna, a beautiful city   x miles.

To Plenorer (? Pianaro).   viii miles.

To Loyan (Logano)   ix miles.

To Florensyl (Firenzola)   vi miles.

To Scarpre   x miles.

To Florence, a very beautiful city   xiiii miles.

To Cassianum (St. Casciano)   v miles.

To Senys (Sienna) a fair city   ix miles.

To Boncovent   xii miles.

To St. Clere   viii miles.   Enquire for an inn. (*Quere pro hospicio Written above the line*)*.

To Redcofyr (? Radicofani)   xii miles.   Here ask the nearer way.

To Aqua pendente   xii miles.

To St. Laurence (St. Lorenzo)   v miles.

To Bulcene (Bolsena)   iii miles.   Outside (*extra*) Bulcene lieth the body of St. Christiana.

To Mownt Flask (Montefiascone)   vi miles.   Good muskadel is made here.

It is said that the body of the glorious Virgin Margaret lieth here.

To Viterbo   viii miles.   Here lieth St. Rosina or Rosa ; and here is a very fine aqueduct, etc.   Get girdles here, please (*Adquire zonas si placet*).

To Sowterys (Sutri)   xii miles.

[1] *The river Po.*

[2] *To cross the river Pamaro.*

*Fo. 42a.

G

To Towrys (Torignano) x miles. Take care now about the inn lest . . . (*cut off by binder*).

Then to the fair city, namely Rome, xiiii miles.

AN ALTERNATIVE ROUTE (ALIA VIA)

Those who do not wish to go through the city of Cologne, on account of (*the tax levied by*) the Bishop, etc. (*sic*),—with God's assistance—can very well travel by this route : namely, from Akon (Aachen) or Aquis, as it is called, to Coldeherbyr (Kalterhberg) is iiii miles.

Then to Zeffryn vi miles and a half.

To Bidbower (? Bittburg) i mile and a half.

To Trivers, or Trier iiii miles. St. Matthias lieth here (*written over the line*).

To Seynt Wayndelyn (Wendel) vii miles.

To Cayserlowter (Kaiserlauten) vii miles.

To Newstat (Neustadt) vii miles.

To Speyer, a beautiful city, iii miles.

Be very careful about accommodation (*hospicio*) on this route, because it is not much used, nevertheless the road is a good one and not very long.

THE EXCHANGE OF DIVERS KINDS OF MONEY [Fo. 42b.]

I William Brewyn, Chaplain, received (*in exchange, for ixs. in English money*), ii ducats in the city of Rome. As I did also for others by means of a letter (of credit) which I received in London, on the Bank of Jacobo de Medici. (*In margin, "garard" xviiid.*). Also for xls, I received xi Rynysh gyldyrnes (guilders) of the Duke of Burgundy, and they bear the image of St. Andrew, the apostle, and these I received at Brygg (Bruges) in the bank there.

For one Rynys gyldyrn (guilder) I received overseas

xxi plakks (*placket*) and for one plak, I received xxiiii mits.

For a Rynysh gyldryn, I received xxiiii colenpens.

For one Cologne penny I received xii hallers.

For one Beme, I received xii feras.

For one gyldryn I received xxi blaffordys (*blaffert, a small coin of Cologne*).

iii plakkys are worth v Cologne pence.

i brasse peny is worth iid halfpenny.

For one lylyard I received iii halfpennies.

For one old groat (*antiquo grosso*) (I received) half a groat and a halfpenny.

For three Phylypp pens, I received v groats.

i Stuffyr or Stater (*stiver*) is worth one plakk and ii pence.

i lely plakke is worth iii halfpence.

i curt is worth ii mits.

i new plakk is worth iiiid.

i old plak is worth iid.

i Stotyr is worth five pence.

And vi Colon pence are worth five stuffyrs. [Fo. 43a.]

vi plankks (*sic*) are worth iii stuffyrs, and so one stuffyr is worth iid.

One lylyard is worth two pence and a halfpenny.

For one bemys I received iii crucers, and the same for i blafford.

For one Karlyn, or papal groat, I received vii beaukos.

For one ducat, I received x Carlyns and iiii beacos (? *bezants*).

For i papal groat, I received iiii bolendyns.

For i bolendyn I received vi feras or vi Kateryns.

For one ducat xxviii Venys grotys.

There are many more kinds of money in use on the route, but these will suffice ; but it should be noted also, that papal groats, or Karlyns, and bemys, or blaffordys, and crucers, are the coins chiefly used ; and that Cologne pence and plakks are in their own places (*where they are current*), particularly serviceable (*proficui*)[1].

*   *   *

(Here a page has been cut out ; but we learn from the Table of Contents, at the beginning of the volume, that here followed an account of a pilgrimage to the Holy Land).

*   *   *

CANTERBURY-RELICS [Fo. 95a.]

These are the bodies of the saints, and the relics in the church of St. Thomas, and Archprelate, in the city of Canterbury :

First, the body of St. Thomas, martyr, and archbishop.

Also, the body of Elphege,   the body of St. Blase,
the body of St. Salvius,   the body of St. Dunstan,
the body of the saint   the body of St. Wilfrid,
who is called Odo,   the body of St. Anselm,
the body of St. Audoen   the body of St. Cuthbert

The bodies of Saints : Athelard, Bregwin, Plegmund, Alfric, Athelgar, Ciric, (*Siric* or *Sigeric*), Vulfred Athelred, Wulfhelm, Celnoth, Fleogild, Athelm, Vulgan, and also the body of the very celebrated virgin Syburgis.

(In the margin is written *Corpora xxiv*).

RELICS

Some of the wood of the Holy Cross of our Lord Jesus Christ.

Three thorns of His triumphal crown.

*Some of His seamless coat.

---

[1]*Profitable* written in the margin.

*The relics marked by an asterisk are not in the Inventory which was made when Henry of Eastry was prior in 1315 and is printed in Legg and Hope's *Inventories of Christ Church, Canterbury.*

Some of the veil of the Blessed Virgin Mary, some of her hair and some of her tomb.

The arm (*brachium*) of St. Symeon, he who received Jesus Christ in his arms (*ulnas*). [Fo. 95b.]

The arm of St. Bartholomew, apostle.

The arm of St. Gregory, pope.

The arm of St. George, martyr, and one of his teeth.

The arm of St. Roman, bishop and confessor.

The arm of St. Wulstan, bishop of Worcester.

The arm of St. Hugh, bishop of Lincoln.

The arm of St. Richard, bishop of Chichester.

*The arm of St. Osmund, bishop of Salisbury, and confessor.

The arm of St. Mildred, virgin.

The thigh bone of one of the Innocents, who were slain instead of Christ, in the time of Herod.

One tooth of St. John the Baptist.

Some of the cross of the Apostle St. Peter.

Some of the cross of the Apostle St. Andrew.

Some of the bones of the apostles Philip and James, and of St. Thomas.

One finger of St. Stephen.

Some of the roasted flesh, and of the gridiron of St. Laurence, the martyr.

Some of the bones of St. Vincent, the martyr, and St. Clement.

One finger of St. Alban.

Some of the bones of St. Sebastian. [Fo. 96a.]

The jawbones of SS. Cosmas and Damian.

Some of the bones of St. Martin.

One tooth of St. Benedict, abbot.

Some of the hairs of St. Mary Magdalene.

*The Alabaster (box) of St. Mary Magdalene.

Some of the bones of St. Katerin, virgin, and some of the oil of the tomb of the same.

*The relics marked by an asterisk are not in the Inventory which was made when Henry of Eastry was prior in 1315 and is printed in Legg and Hope's *Inventories of Christ Church, Canterbury.*

Also, the head of St. Furse, confessor.

Also, the head of Austroberta, virgin.

Also, the vestments of St. Thomas, the martyr, in which he lay buried L years.

Some of the brain of the same St. Thomas.

The head of St. Blaise, the martyr, who is said to have suffered at Sebaste in Capadocia, together with the shoulder blade of the same martyr, whose glorious body Plegmund, an eminent Archprelate of the church, after incessant labours, by leave of Pope Formosus, caused to be brought from the city of Rome, to this see of our world (*ad hanc nostri orbis sedem*), where it was placed in an honourable position —behind the high altar—and between the shrines of Saints Dunstan and Elphege[1]. [Fo. 96b.]

Also, note the following inscription :

" To those persons who shall make an offering at the high altar of this church, where of old time these relics were kept, or shall say the Lord's Prayer, or other prayers devoutly, a great indulgence is granted, to wit one of xxix years and lxxxxvi days."

Also, note that the sum of the indulgences of the whole church is $\underset{\text{xxxvii}}{\text{M}}$.. years liii (37053) years and cc and l (250) days in perpetuity.

In the year of the Lord mcccclxx, that is to say, in the year of the Jubilee of the same Thomas, the martyr, I William Brewyn, Chaplain, was present at the time, to wit, on the feast of the translation of the same St. Thomas, the martyr, and wrote what is described above.

I give thanks to the Lord Jesus and Holy Mary.

[1]In the inventory of 1315, which was drawn up during the priorate of Henry of Eastry, the head of St. Blaise is said to be " in the great reliquary cupboard near the high altar " ; like the heads of SS. Furse and Austroberta it was enclosed in a silver-gilt case (*in capite argenteo deaurato*) (Inventories of Ch. Ch. Cant. Legg and Hope, p. 80).

Notice also the stone-head of the heretic, standing before St. Anselm, in the chapel.

Notatur de capite lapideo heretici coram sancto Anselmo in Capella. Item de pomo sancti Thome. William Somner in his Antiquities of Canterbury (1640)—after describing the verses in the stained glass windows of the north aisle of the choir, adds four others, which, he states, were "legible of late on the wall of the north ile of the Quire, almost at the foot of the painted piece there (? *The legend of St. Eustace*) and do contain a brief dialogue between St. Anselm sometime Archbishop here, and an heretike about the virgin conception of our blessed Lady, written (it there appears) Anno Domini 1477.

Haereticus :   "Nunquam Natura mutavit sic sua jura,
               Ut virgo pareret, ni virginitate careret.
Anselmus :   "Lumine solari nescit vitrum violari
               Nec vitrum sole, nec virgo puerpera prole."

[Translation]

Heretic :   Nature is constant, no man can believe
               That a pure virgin could a child conceive.
Anselm :   The sun's ray sullies not the window pane,
               Nor need child-bearing a pure virgin stain.

Also, the pome of St. Thomas (? *Adam's apple*).

POEMS [Fo. 98a.]
(To the Blessed Virgin Mary)
Speciosa facta es & suavis & cet.

Thou holy moder off God Almygth,
By special grace off hys divinite,
Thou art mad specious and swete bothe beutius and
    brygth,
In ye delicys off thin virginte,
(W)hom verily seeyng, cordyng to myn tale,
The dowters off Syon vernant[1] in lusty colower,
In flowers off rosys and lelys off ye vale
To sey martirs and Virgyns off heavenly bower,
Off alle blyssyd creaturs as holy chyrch techyd,
More and moste blyssyd I certen zow fful suyr[2],
Martirs and virgyns wt al seynts hyr hath prechyd,
Preysyng hyr[3] quenys thei ded her besy cuyr[4].

[1]Flourishing.   [2]Sure.   [3]Their.   [4]Cure.

Gaude Virgo Mater

Joy thu virgyn as it is ryzth,   (*gaudium*
The fader off hevyn he lovid the(e) welle,   *in margin*)
Ye angel gabriel off blys so brygth
He sent to the(e) tydynggs to telle.
Make thou mery as seyd is be forn[1].
The secund person in trinite
In flesshe and blood was off ye born,
Bothe god and man in verite.
Joy thu lady and virgyn brygth,
Thow thine son deyd on tree.
Resyn he is by hys owne myth[2]
Deth destroyd, and mad(e) us free.
Virgyn whyt as lely flower [Fo. 98b.]
Joy thu hartyly, ffor truth it is
Thin son ascendyd to ye tower
Of(f) ye rych kyngdom off blys
Lady off virtu and devocion,
Exaltyd be forn ye trinite
Of(f) angell off lyzth be mene[3] of thei son
Joy thorw evere yer for to be.

Gaude flore virginali

1. Joy thu Mary wt virgyn flower,
   In honour special for thin levyng,
   Transcendyng angell off hevyn tower,
   In trone by thy son in hevyn syttyng.
   Joy dere spowse off God Almyzth.
   Ffor he lyst the(e) so to calle.

2. In this warld thu art so bryzt,
   Thou pacyst[4] ye lyztts alle.
   Joy thu vessel off virtu clere,
   At thin wyl al is pendent,

3. Al hool[5] ye celestial cure.
   Beuyous[6] moder happy and reverent
   Joy thu virgyn and be glad

---

[1]Before.   [2]Might.   [3]By means.   [4]Surpasseth.
[5]Whole.   [6]Beauteous.

4. Of(f) swete thu thin sonn to see,
   Of(f) (w)hom thin wyl al shal be had
   Ffor (w)hom thu prayest savyd to be.
   Joy thu moder off wrechys[1] hard [Fo. 100a.]

5. That the(e) warchyp here I wys
   Ye fadyr off hevyn hem reward,
   Both here and efte[2] in blys.
   Joy virgyn make, syttyng in see,

6. To thin meryts acordyng evyn,
   Exalted neyxte ye trinite,
   Above alle odyrs that arn[3] in hevyn.
   Joy thu moder off al clemesse.[4]

7. Certeyn suyrd wt out lesyng[5]
   That thes joyes bothe more and lesse
   To the(e) shal ben everlastyng.

[*The Magi*]

The Sterre shoon bothe nyzt and day
To laid three kynges yr ower lord lay,
Truth it is ful sekyrly[6]
Three kynggs that were ful reverent,
That sowth[7] ihu ryzth besyly
With holy devcocion and good intent.
A ryzth fayer sterre to them dede peer,
Ful orient in hys shynyng,
That browt hem forth all in feer
To Jer(usa)l(e)m to here tydyng.
Ther thei askyd wt or consent.
Wher is he that now born is
Kyng off jwys verament[8] ? [Fo. 100b.]
Hym to seeke it is ow[r] blys,
Just it is as trewlove knot
Hys ster wee seyn in est ful brygth,
Hym to worshyp wyth all ow[r] thowth[9],

---

[1]Wretches. [2]Hereafter. [3]are. [4]Kindness. [5]Lying.
[6]Certainly. [7]Sought. [8]Really, truly. [9]Thought, attention.

Here we come as it is rygth.
Kyng herrowd wt thys wex wode[1],
And dede seke up ye prophicye,
He thout hym sore to swage[2] his blode
And zif it were trowth than he shulde deye.
Thou bethlem in jwys land
In iury princs thu art not leest,
For out of the(e) a duke shal fond[3]
Israel to rewyl myn pepyl best,
Thus seyd y[e] prophecye in wrytyng swyr[4]
Off Jhu Cryst off (w)hom I syng,
That off jewys he shulde be kyng.
Trublyd than was wt outyn leese
Kyng herrowd thys heryng,
And al jer(usa)l(e)m hym to pleese,
Ryzt sore hem grevyd swych tydyng.
All principalle prestys he dede present,
And scribys of ye pepul that thei were there,
Off Cryste berth to say her[5] intent,
Ryzth as her books dede hem lere[6],
Than herrowd ful priuilyche [Fo. 101a.]
The kyngg he clepyd[7] that diligently
The tyme off yesterr thei shuld hym teche
To hem that apperyd so propyrly,
Whan all he her' hartys wyst[8],
Sendyng hem forth he precept
Diligently goo atte zow[r] lyst[9],
And aske afftyr ye chyld wt outyn lette,
But whan that chelde ze have cum tylle
Comth ageyn and tellye me,
That I hysm wirchyp may at wylle,
As it perteynith to myn degree.
Thus he spake wel serpentyne[10],
Wt gret sorrow and mekyl[11] smerte.

[1]Wrathful, mad.   [2]Shed.   [3]Found.   [4]Sure.
[5]Their   [6]Learn   [7]Proclaimed   [8]Knew
[9]Where you will   [10]Cunningly   [11]Much

For he than hopyd to see ye tyme
Tha the shuld stryk ye chyld to herte.
Thus whan thei ye kyng had harde
They redyn her way as it was beste.
See the sterre thei seey afterwarde
Ryzth hem precedyng in ye este.
And when ye sterre thei had in syzte[1]
Mery thei were and mad(e) gret glee.
Lost thei nevir that ich lyzt[2]
Tyl thei come where thei wuld bee.
In to the house than thei entryng
Fond thei there that semely sygth,
Ye chyld Jhu ow^r hevyn Kyng
Wt Mary hys modyr ow^r lady brygth.
They fel prostat wt reverence
Upon heir knese, semly to see.
Gold myrr and frankincens [Fo. 101b.]
To hym offryd ich[3] off ye thre
Whan thei her offryng thus had mad(e),
Answer in sleep receyvyd ful playn,
Al anoder way to hem ful of glad.
But not to herrowd turnyd thei agayn.
Thankyn God in trinite,
Wyth joy and myrth everlastynge,
Sore thei come hom(e) to her cuntree.
Thus was her pylgrimage brouth to ende.
Than wex herrowd in wroth ful grylle[4]
He gruggyd[5] he gronyd[6] he cried full felle
That ye kynggs come not hym (to) tylle.
Where fore feel[7] chyldyr dede he qwelle.
For in her dethe he put hys trost
That cryst shuld dey be gret resoun[8]
Zif thei were slayn in every coost,
And specialy in bethlem toun.
But zet he sped not off hys pray
King herrowd that gryme lyer.

[1]Sight [2]Same light. [3]Each. [4]Fearful. [5]murmured
[6]Groaned. [7]Feeble. [8]That Christ would be certain to die.

But he to helle hath take hys way
Ever ther to dwelle in peynful fyer.
Innocents by grace martyrs zyng
To hevyn were born wt angell brygth,
Ther to be cround of ow[r] hevenly kyng
God bryng us alle to that ich[1] lygth,
Wher we may joy wt ow[r] kyng
Wt seynts and angells everych one
The face off very God both trine and one
I thank now God myn song is done.

THE STONING OF STEPHEN.

[Fo. 99a.]

[The first part is missing]

*   *   *

The prince of prests to hym gan say
Arn those now trew wyth out (en)les(e)
To hym stevyn answeryd nay,
Hym wel excusyng be fayer processe,
In wych wt resonys ryth pregnant
The lawe he provyd, wt tempyl holye
And god wt moyses hys servant
Hym self for them redy to deye.
But sharply he spak(e) and wyth effect,
And perfectly kept his charite,
That her gret synnys thei shuld correct,
And grace receyve if it wyld be.
Whan thei had hard hys holy fyt[2]
For cursydnesse thei were nere wode[3].
Ryt gret malyce her harts were kyt[4]
Some hem thowth to sheed hys blood.
Thei staryd thei mokkyd wt face frunyng
Her harts so hatyd goddys clarke.

[1]Same.   [2]Speech.   [3]Mad.   [4]Cut.

Her tethe hei ierryd[1] wt gret gruggyng,
O sathanas this was thin warke !
Whan wt ye holy gost verei
Replete was stevyn intendyng blys[2]
The glory of God certeyn he sey [Fo. 99b.],
And ihu standyng a dextris[3]
And thus he seyd, to (w)hom I wyss,
Behold I se in thys seson
Hevenes opund to me of blyss,
And on ye ryt hand ye maydnys son,
Stondyng zet of Godds virtu,
As hoo shuld sey wyth owtyn zelpe[4]
Redy to me trosty and tro,
Zow to confund and me to helpe.
Whan thes were he seyd wtout lesyng
Wt gret voyce thei cryed out,
Stopte her eers, on hym sawtyng[5]
To gedyr thei wrowt round about.
They drevyn hym out of yt cete.
Like as cryste in his passione,
Tyl they come (where) thei wuld be
Where her clothes thei reft of(f) sone.
A zyng[6] man that was of worthynes
That tyme saule but now paul hyte[7]
The clothys he kepte of ye testes[8]
Leyd but lytyl from hys fete.
These men than toke stonys in hast [Fo. 97a.],
Rygth gret ryt sharp and also round,
Up on stevyn wyth streyngthe thei cast
Hym to dryve down to ye ground.
Thus wyth stonys thei beat down stevyn,
Standyng in prayers that he dede make :
" Lord ihu," thus was it evyn,
" Myn sowle myn spryt I may the(e) take."
Than stevyn hese knees on ground down sette
To pray for hys enmyes wul he not blynne[9]

[1]Gnashed, or to make a gnashing sound, the earliest example in O.E.D. is from Skelton, A.D. 1525. [2]In expectation of bliss. [3]at his right hand. [4]Boast. [5]Leaping. [6]Young. [7]Hight—called, named. [8]Witnesses. [9]Cease.

Lor(d) ihu cryst wt voyce grette,
He seyth, sette not thus to hem non synne,
Whyl thus he prayed thei brosde¹ hys fleshe,
His bones thei brake ye blood out leepe,
Of this scripteur beryth wytenesse,
He in ower lord hath take hys sleepe
He slepyth in hope now note wel thys,
Sacrifyse of love he offryd ryt.
He deyth not that gooth to blys,
The prests confoundyd wt gret hate
This martyrs bod for to reste,
At ier(usa)l(e) mwt out ye gate [Fo. 97b.],
To be devourynd wt foule and beeste.
But he to (w)hom hys feyth and love
Truly he kept in hys levyng²
Angell hym sent from hevyn above,
That suyrly hym kept from all hurtyng
Gamalyel wt rape³ privie,
To thys martir compacient,
XX mylis fro that citye,
His body beryd in hys moment⁴
But now this precious perle so brygth
That first in martyrs lede ye daunce
Zif ze wyl fynd hym ful ryt
He lyth at rome wt seynt laurance⁵
Sevyn persones from deth to lyve
He restoryd, it is no fabyl.
Ever hys myracklys were so ryve
That thei arn innumerabyl
O good ihu for this knyth⁶
Graunte us grace to come to hevyn,
And make us partyners of that lygth
Where evyr we may regne wt steven.

---

¹Bruised.   ²Believing.   ³With speed privily.   ⁴Monument
⁵*See* Fo. 35a   ⁶Knight.

INDEX

SAINTS   Page